CW00522603

Generation Z D

Key concepts and ideas for the next
generation of developers

Dinis Cruz

Generation Z Developers

Key concepts and ideas for the next generation of developers

Dinis Cruz

This work is licensed under a Creative Commons Attribution 4.0 International License

Contents

CONTENTS

GitHub Issues

All content related to this book is hosted at the GitHub DinisCruz/-Book_Generation_Z_Developer[1] repo.

This repo not only contains all text (in Markdown), but also all pending issues and ideas[2]. I'm using the exact workflow and ideas presented in this book in the development of this book :)

You can read more about GitHub and Git in the respective chapters, but if you want to be involved in an open source and Creative Commons project, this would be a good place to start.

Here are the current list of issues (as of the last time this book was generated) that you can help out

Issues list

Using GitHub api on **08 Oct 2018** the following **5** issues had the **show-in-book** label:

- Add chapter on 'cloud-native' : #6[3]
- Add chapter on 'Typography and Design' : #5[4]
- Add chapter on 'Closure' : #4[5]
- Re-apply context fixes submitted to Build repo : #3[6]
- Add chapter on 'Coordinated Disclosure' : #2[7]

---

[1]https://github.com/DinisCruz/Book_Generation_Z_Developer
[2]https://github.com/DinisCruz/Book_Generation_Z_Developer/issues
[3]https://api.github.com/repos/DinisCruz/Book_Generation_Z_Developer/issues/6
[4]https://api.github.com/repos/DinisCruz/Book_Generation_Z_Developer/issues/5
[5]https://api.github.com/repos/DinisCruz/Book_Generation_Z_Developer/issues/4
[6]https://api.github.com/repos/DinisCruz/Book_Generation_Z_Developer/issues/3
[7]https://api.github.com/repos/DinisCruz/Book_Generation_Z_Developer/issues/2

Generation Z
Developers

Introduction

Hi Generation Z Developer, if you are one and want to learn as much as you can about your craft, this is the book for you.

I decided to write this book after doing a series of presentations to Gen Z audiences. As part of this process I discovered gaps in your generation's understanding of the history behind a number of key ideas and technologies that underpin the technological revolution that we are the in middle of. I also wanted to share a number of real-world concepts, practices and technologies that will make you a much better and effective professional in today's highly competitive tech world.

Here is the slide that started it all in 2017, how many logos do you recognize?

The presentation started with me asking the audience if the logos looked familiar. I soon realised that, not only did the audience not recognize most of the logos, they didn't know the history behind them. More importantly, the audience didn't understand the story behind **why** they where created nor they were aware of the problem (or itch) they originally looked to address.

Why is the **why** important? All of these icons were 'catalysts for change'. It is important to understand the history behind them, why they occurred and the change they drove. Each one of these icons changed the world of technology, and created paradigms shifts that still impact our world today.

For example, one of the really significant innovations was the creation of the Creative Commons license - an adaption of a traditional copyright license. This was one of my initial *'WFT! you don't know what Creation Commons is???'* realizations.

Creative Commons licensing gives a number of rights to the consumer of creations (rather than the originator of a creation holding onto the rights). It allows ideas, creations and concepts to spread easily and without limitation.

This book is released under a 'Creative Commons Attribution 4.0 International License'. This license means, amongst other things, that you are free (as in 'entitled to') to use all the material and content from this book. The only requirement on your part being around acknowledgement of the author and source attribution. You can even sell other books and any derived work based on the content from this book.

Fundamentally, the freedom of knowledge isn't a new idea but the real impact of Creative Commons was about how it became applied to technology, an industry often dominated solely by commercial interests. For better or worse, the closed approach has shaped the technology and systems that dominate the world today. As you will see through the book, what I find interesting is not a particular technology or idea, but the ways in which those ideas change how we act, think and behave.

We are in the middle of a massive technological and cultural revolution and you have the opportunity to decide if you want to be a pawn, a player or even a play-maker in this new world. By understanding the history, thinking and mechanics of this change you will be in the best position to adapt and thrive. If you don't understand the past, you are not only bound to repeat its mistakes but also miss opportunities you may not even be aware of.

Please join me in this interesting trip down memory lane, where I will try to explain how I understand and learned from a multitude number of technologies, ideas and events.

Be involved and contribute

If you have never contributed to an Open Source (or Creative Commons) project, then how about using this book as your first experiments?

You can find all content for this book in this GitHub repo[8] and you can submit ideas and issues (you found when reading this book) here[9]

Please share your views, suggestions and criticisms and don't hesitate to reach out to me on @DinisCruz[10]

Generation Z

Generation Z is the generation born after 1996[11]. Like all generation boundaries, their differences may be generalized and there will always be exceptions to this rule. That said, when viewed constructively, it represents an interesting mix of great values and digital capabilities.

The older members of this generation (at the time of writing, 2018) are about 22 years old. They don't remember the 9/11 attackers, were 11 when the first iPhone came out (2007) and are the first real 'born online' generation. In parts of the world that are privileged enough to enjoy ubiquitous access to technology, many members of this generation have not experienced a world without ready access

---

[8]https://github.com/DinisCruz/Book_Generation_Z_Developer
[9]https://github.com/DinisCruz/Book_Generation_Z_Developer/issues
[10]https://twitter.com/DinisCruz
[11]https://twitter.com/PaoliCGPI/status/961121404048601088

to the internet on some kind of device. This is the generation that is entering the job market right now.

I have personal experience of this generation, I have two daughters currently aged 13 and 15, and I have also been professionally involved in a number of projects focused on Generation Z. I've run sessions teaching UK high school kids how to 'hack' (in the ethical rather than illegal sense of the word) and even younger developers how to code so they would be able to apply their skills in real world scenarios.

I'm focusing on Generation Z because I believe they've missed the historical understanding of a number of key technological revolutions required to be competitive in the market place. At the current pace of technological advancement so much history can be taken for granted. Without a full understanding of the past, we only learn from shadows and curated versions of reality.

I'm worried about Gen Z

Although Generation Z has some spectacular traits and values, I occasionally perceive a lack of intellectual curiosity that worries me. This is arguably the most tolerant and diversity-aware generation. But, having grown up with an innate acceptance of the technology around us, many of the building blocks of today's technology stacks are simply assumed to be ever present. Much like driving a car or flying a plane with no knowledge of the engineering involved.

This is a huge advantage in a sense; many of the older generation perceived boundaries don't inhibit Generation Z. By the same token however, even more opportunities can come from understanding the origin, history and evolution of the technology journey so far.

This is an age when information and knowledge is often a Google search away. Yet, conversation after conversation I've found - perhaps unsurprisingly - that Generation Z teenagers have a very superficial understanding of the history that underpins the technologies they use. How and why this technology came to be in the first place and the original problems it tried to solve.

My hope with this book is to fill these gaps and provide context and references to inform and enable better decision making. This is very important because they are the generation will need to save the world from the mess previous generations have created.

Overwhelming curiosity

How will I know if this book has succeded? I'm hopeful that the reader can enjoy a few moments of overwhelming curiosity and go on learning more about a certain topic. Moments when you follow link after link about a particular topic, and think 'WOW, that is fr**** awesome!'.

If you are lucky enough to find yourself in this place, congratulations! You just found 'the zone'. An amazing mental place where you have the chance to be single minded and 100% absorbed. This is the best way to learn.

Whenever you find yourself in this headspace, dont stop! Follow it as long as your brain allows it, and don't stop for anything. Social events, eating and sleeping can always wait (more or less; respect your physical and mental health and never take them for granted). The 'zone' is a magical place to be, so learn to recognize when you find yourself inside it, and use it to explore as much as you can.

How to get a job

One of my objectives with this book is to help you to find a great job. One that you will love going to everyday; one where you are in for a steep learning curve and one that aligns what you are passionate about with what your employer is happy to pay for.

It is very important to realise that if you are in a job (or school) where your learning curve is not off-the-charts, you are short-changing your life and your career. Nobody cares as much about your career as you do, and you are the only one that has full control over your attitude to learning. You can chose everyday on how engaged and receptive you are to learn and to be taught by others. It is not exaggeration to say that you decide your future's direction and path with every decision you make.

There is a lot of competition out there and if you look at what is coming next, namely AI and the next billion internet users, you'll need to maximise your chances and opportunities.

I really like the Gen Z realization that a job is something that should be rewarding and not just a way to make money. After all, the best job is when you are paid to do something that you would do for free. Although I am very fortunate to be in that situation, where I love my job and what I do every day, it didn't happened by accident. I made a number of key decisions in my life, some with very short-term negative implications, that allowed me to align what I love to do with what the market wants to pay.

Being passionate and loving your job

Find what you are passionate for, what you really care about and align your career with those ideas. The best part is that this is a massive win-win situation, since the more passionate you are about a particular topic, the more you care about it, and the more valuable you are to the company that is employing you.

Having one competitive advantage

The best way to get a job is to have ONE competitive advantage. One activity or task that you can do better than the person or company hiring you. For example in the 1990s for a lot of companies it was simply that you could use a computer! In the 2000s is was using the Internet. In the early days of software development or security, all it took was good programming or hacking experience. Although it might look that the bar was lower those days, the reality is that those who could do it were the ones who proactively embraced the technologies and learned them against all odds. Individuals can become experts at new technology faster than the tech companies. You can be first in line for a job when they need that expertise. These days, it is technologies and ideas like (all covered in this book):

- ML/AI
- Graphs
- Chaos Engineering
- GitHub
- Git
- Jira
- Creative Commons Licences
- Continuous Integration
- AWS
- WallabyJs

Own your career development

You are the one in charge of your career. Yes, listen to advice but only you can ultimately choose which paths to follow. You need to discover those paths by yourself, via trial and error, and a great way to do that is to work for companies who are aligned with those paths.

And how do you start working with those companies?

Easy, start collaborating on their Open Source projects. Act like you are part of the company. Understand their values, and behave in ways that will add value to that company, namely the tech stack.

Start by approaching the key individuals and developers from those companies and communities, both offline and online, in a way that adds value to them. Build relationships that will teach you a lot, and potentially lead to very interesting job offers, or at least references. Start by learning how to add value and how to become good at proactively solving problems, which is one of the most valuable assets you can bring to a company.

What's interesting is that there is nothing stopping you from doing this! We are in very open, collaborative and creative times. You have nothing to lose by giving it all you've got, and everything to gain.

How this book is being created

This book is being created using the principles and technologies described in this book :)

- All content is available under an CC License (Creative Commons)
- Markdown is used to write the content
- All content is managed using git and published under an public GitHub repository
- GitHub Issues are used to track bugs, issues and ideas
- Leanpub is used to create and publish the digital versions of this book
- Content is being published early and often on Leanpub and on some blogs (to share the ideas, get feedback and build community)

If you have never used git, github or markdown, why don't you help out in the creation of this book? You can do this by opening up issues with your feedback on the ideas and content (I really value those comments since it helps me to make sure the content makes sense to the target audience)

MVP for Gen Z Dev

This section will try to define what should be the MVP for a Generation Z Developer.

MVP is a term used regularly in the software development industry to mean Minimum Viable Product[12], and it represents the minimum set of features and capabilities that a particular product/release/version should have in order to add value to the end users/customers.

From a Gen Z Dev point of view (i.e. you the reader), the technologies and workflows described in this section are key to make you highly productive and effective team player.

Although you might not use them all in your day-to-day activities, it is very important to understand what they are and why they where created in the first place.

In this section I will try to give you ideas on practical steps you can take, and here is first one:

> TASK: Write blog posts with your experiments and challenges in understanding and using these ideas, technologies or workflows.

Drop me a link to these posts so that you have at least one reader :)

Note: Best way to do it is via a twitter mention (i.e. tweet with a link to the article and my twitter handle tag @DinisCruz)

---

[12]https://en.wikipedia.org/wiki/Minimum_viable_product

Creative Commons

Deciding which license you choose to share your work with is one of the most important decisions you make in your professional life.

You can either go down a path where you think everything you create (outside paid work) is super precious and needs protecting or you soon realise that your ability to think about ideas, and (more importantly) to execute upon those ideas, is extremely valuable.

Often, with the former approach you may be afraid that your ideas will be copied so you don't share them. In the latter approach you are happy to share your ideas as much as possible.

The best way to share your ideas and way of thinking is to release your content and ideas under a Creative Commons Copyright License

So what is Creative Commons (CC)?

Let's start by looking at the definition of Creative Commons[13] from Wikipedia:

> A Creative Commons (CC) license is one of several public copyright licenses that enable the free distribution of an otherwise copyrighted work. A CC license is used when an author wants to give people the right to share, use, and build upon a work that they have created. CC provides an author flexibility (for example, they might choose to allow only non-commercial uses of their own work) and protects the people who use or redistribute an author's work from concerns of copyright infringement as long as they abide by the conditions that are specified in the license by which the author distributes the work

Basically, this license defines the rules of the game that are applied to the content that you publish. By releasing your content under

---

[13]https://en.wikipedia.org/wiki/Creative_Commons

this license (and your code under Open Source) you are sending a strong message of your values and positioning. You are also maximizing the potential for your ideas to be far reaching and impactful. Like Steve Jobs said in his Stanford Commencement address[14] in 2005 *"...you can't connect the dots looking forward; you can only connect them looking backward. So you have to trust that the dots will somehow connect in your future..."* , you could be generating a number of opportunities for your future self, or you could even be teaching something to your future self (it's amazing how much we forget over time)

Creative Commons license variations and this book

This book is released under the Creative Commons Attribution 4.0 International (CC BY 4.0)[15] which defines the following terms (see website):

You are free to:

- Share — copy and redistribute the material in any medium or format
- Adapt — remix, transform, and build upon the material for any purpose, even commercially.

Under the following terms: - Attribution — You must give appropriate credit, provide a link to the license, and indicate if changes were made. You may do so in any reasonable manner, but not in any way that suggests the licensor endorses you or your intended use as licensee.

The licensor cannot revoke these freedoms as long as you follow the license terms.

[14]https://news.stanford.edu/2005/06/14/jobs-061505/
[15]https://creativecommons.org/licenses/by/4.0/deed.en_US

No additional restrictions — You may not apply legal terms or technological measures that legally restrict others from doing anything the license permits.

Although all CC licenses allow content to be shared, some have more restrictions:

- **Attribution-ShareAlike** 4.0 - need to attribute and use the same CC license (this has a 'viral' effect since it forces changes to also have a CC license)
- **Attribution-NoDerivatives** 4.0 - need to attribute and prohibits the sharing of adaptations of the material
- **Attribution-NonCommercial-NoDerivatives** 4.0 - need to attribute, prohibits sharing of adaptations of the material and requires approval/permission from the rights holder before being permitted to be used commercially

I don't like the licenses above since they put restrictions on how the content can be used (which is against my views of sharing) but for companies or individuals that are new to CC, these are good first steps.

For reference here is a table which shows the various types of Creative Commons licenses:

Icon ◆	Description ◆	Acronym ◆	Allows Remix culture ◆	Allows commercial use ◆	Allows Free Cultural Works ◆	Meets 'Open Definition' ◆
PUBLIC DOMAIN	Freeing content globally without restrictions	CC0	Yes	Yes	Yes	Yes
CC BY	Attribution alone	BY	Yes	Yes	Yes	Yes
CC BY SA	Attribution + ShareAlike	BY-SA	Yes	Yes	Yes	Yes
CC BY NC	Attribution + Noncommercial	BY-NC	Yes	No	No	No
CC BY NC SA	Attribution + Noncommercial + ShareAlike	BY-NC-SA	Yes	No	No	No
CC BY ND	Attribution + NoDerivatives	BY-ND	No	Yes	No	No
CC BY NC ND	Attribution + Noncommercial + NoDerivatives	BY-NC-ND	No	No	No	No

[16]

---

[16]https://en.wikipedia.org/wiki/Creative_Commons_license

Obscurity is your biggest threat

Tim O'Reilly on Piracy is Progressive Taxation, and Other Thoughts on the Evolution of Online Distribution[17] provides this amazing quite: *'For a typical author, obscurity is a far greater threat than piracy.'*.

What this means is that you have more to lose by not publishing your ideas, music, or art.

Creative Commons is changing science

Ironically, the majority of modern science was built on the principle of sharing ideas, cross-verification and healthy challenges of assumptions/theories. But for a while, science (due to a number of reasons) started to become a closed world, with large amounts of information and data only being available to a selected few.

Good news is, in the last decade this has started to change. I think a big part of it was caused by the cross fertilization of practices brought to science by developers who were exposed to the Open Source workflow (and culture and effectiveness) and help to push for a much more open and collaborative environment between teams. See for example the collaboration of code and data-sets that is happening on areas like cancer research.

Also, amazing is the massive amount of data that is being shared today by government agencies. See these books for amazing infographics created from this data:

- Information is Beautiful[18]
- Visualize This: The FlowingData Guide to Design, Visualization, and Statistics[19]

---

[17]http://www.openp2p.com/pub/a/p2p/2002/12/11/piracy.html

[18]https://www.amazon.co.uk/Information-Beautiful-New-David-McCandless/dp/0007492898

[19]https://www.amazon.co.uk/Visualize-This-FlowingData-Visualization-Statistics/dp/0470944889

- Knowledge is Beautiful [20]

See the https://data.gov.uk/ website for data-sets provided by the UK Government (released under the Open Government Licence[21] which is compatible with Creative Commons Attribution License 4.0)

It is key that you learn how to play in this world where massive amounts of data is available. Increasingly so, there is a moral and technical argument that all data created by government should be released under a Creative Commons license, and all code paid by the government should be released under an open source license. Think about the implications that this would have on industries and professions that rely on data to make decisions.

The importance of creating commercially viable models

Note that this doesn't mean that there should not be any financial return from sharing your ideas or content.

I'm a big believer that for any trend to scale and become sustainable, there needs to be a working economic and financial model behind those open workflows.

Basically, authors should be paid for their work.

Also, it is key that the operational teams that support those authors are also paid (for example Wikipedia or Mozilla have highly skilled and well paid professionals working as employees).

Sometimes the payment is hard cash (i.e. the authors/teams are paid to create that content). Sometimes the 'payment' happens in terms of: future opportunities, personal development or karma points (i.e. doing the right thing or sharing knowledge with others the same way it was shared with you).

---

[20]https://www.amazon.co.uk/Knowledge-Beautiful-David-McCandless/dp/0007427921
[21]http://www.nationalarchives.gov.uk/doc/open-government-licence/version/3/

One of the big myths behind open source and Creative Commons is that its authors are all working for free in their bedroom by amateurs. In reality most of the value is created during paid jobs, by highly skilled professionals, with companies supporting the creation of the released code or content.

It is harder than it looks

Don't let your perception prevent you from publishing content you deem of little value. This Impostor Syndrome effect can be very damaging and paralyzing, and you need to take a pragmatic view of what would happen if you do share.

- If what you wrote is not that interesting or valuable to others, then you will have a small number of readers but will have gained valuable knowledge and experience which you can use to help you write your next publication
- If what you have created does get some readers and more importantly, feedback or comments, then you gained a bit and moved the needle a little bit (remember that it is all about incremental gains, and there is no such thing as 'overnight success')

The bottom line is: publishing your research under a CC license is harder than it looks.

You actually have to do it, and remember that taking the first step is often the hardest part.

Doing that journey under a Creative Commons path, means that you have shifted your paradigm from closed to open. It means that you now view your value as someone who can execute ideas (and is happy to share your creations).

Anybody can have ideas, execution is the hard part.

Align your future with Creative Commons

Finally, when choosing which company to work for, take into account their current Creative Commons and Open Source strategy culture for internally developed technology ideas. This should have an impact on your choices.

In most companies, only a very small part of what they create should be closed and proprietary. The rest should released under open licenses.

Remember that in these modern times, especially in technology, it is not uncommon to change jobs regularly. You really want to make sure you still have access to those ideas and code when you move; there is nothing more soul-destroying than having to re-do something you have already created or not having access to good ideas you had in the past.

Open Source

The first thing to learn about Open Source[22] is that it is not just a licence to release software or a way to get code for free (as in no cost).

Open Source is a way of thinking about code and applications, in a way that there isn't an explicit 'lock-in' on the user by the creator. When code is released under an Open Source license, the consumer of that code (namely the developer) gains a number of very important freedoms which have been proven to create very effective and powerful development environments.

You use Open Source applications and code everyday, can you name them?

There is nothing you can do today on the Internet that doesn't touch some Open Source code, and the amount of code that is currently

---

[22]https://opensource.org/

available to you under an Open Source is insane.

An Open Source licence is a copyright license that gives you the right to access, modify and distribute source code. This is a variation of what has been called an Copyleft[23] license. Copyleft is actually an Copyright license based on the idea of giving away rights to the user, instead of the most common use of Copyright, which takes right's away.

Think and behave in an Open Source way

As with the Creative Commons license, Open Source is a way of thinking and behaving about code.

You as a developer should be releasing everything you do with an Open Source license. This will make sure that your 'future self' can still access that code, while maximizing the potential usage and exposure of that code.

You should also be an active contributor to Open Source projects!

Not only you will learn a lot, that participation can really help you in finding a job.

If you are able to get your code changes approved and merged into the code-based of popular Open Source projects, you show the world the quality of your work and communication skills. I can guarantee to you that adding to your CV mentions of these contributions will immediately give you a lot of respect by your peers and interviewees. In fact a great way to get a job in a company is to contribute to an Open Source project hosted by that company.

---

[23]https://en.wikipedia.org/wiki/Copyleft

Who uses Open Source

As you can see from the image above just about everybody is using Open Source these days, on all sorts of industries and use cases. Even Microsoft who used to call Open Source a cancer[24], eventually changed paradigm and now claims to 'love linux'[25] and has recently bought GitHub[26].

History

Open Source is an idea created 20 years ago (in a meeting on February 3rd, 1998) with a number of heavy weights of the Free Software movement, who had the objective to create a common language and framework (and license) to be used by the community.

---

[24]https://web.archive.org/web/20011108013601/http://www.suntimes.com/output/tech/cst-fin-micro01.html
[25]https://cloudblogs.microsoft.com/windowsserver/2015/05/06/microsoft-loves-linux/
[26]https://blogs.microsoft.com/blog/2018/06/04/microsoft-github-empowering-developers/

This lead to the creation of the Open Source Initiative[27] who approves multiple community created Open Source Licenses[28].

One of the challenges that the Open Source license tried to address, was the more aggressive and viral nature of the GPL[29] (General Public License). GPL requires that the developer's release under the same GPL license, all code that uses or modifies the original GPL code.

Basically, once you add some GPL code to you app, you also need to release that app under GPL. In practice this proved to be to restrictive to the adoption of lots of libraries and applications. Even worse, that limitation went against what most Open Source creators want, which is the wide and seamless use of their code

Here is an definition of Open Source software[30] from Wikipedia:

> *Open-source software (OSS) is a type of computer software whose source code is released under a license in which the copyright holder grants users the rights to study, change, and distribute the software to anyone and for any purpose. Open-source software may be developed in a collaborative public manner*

If you look at the arc of history, there is a tendency for code to be open, even when there are massive forces that don't want that (i.e. the companies selling proprietary/closed-source software).

In addition to efficiency, innovation, reduced lock-in and better collaboration, Security is one of the reasons we need the code to be open.

At least when code is open and available, we have the ability to check what is going on, and be much more effective when reviewing

---

[27]https://opensource.org/
[28]https://en.wikipedia.org/wiki/Open-source_license
[29]https://en.wikipedia.org/wiki/GNU_General_Public_License
[30]https://en.wikipedia.org/wiki/Open-source_software

its security (see Reflections on Trusting Trust[31] for more on trust chains).

Note that this doesn't mean that Open Source software is auto-magically secure just by being Open Source (we still need an ecosystem that rewards or pays for security reviews and secure development practices)

Another major evolution in the history of open source was its effect on companies like Google and Facebook, where Open Source applications and code where a major contributor to their scalability and success.

Open source business models

It is amazing to see the change in the industry and thinking around Open Source. In early days of Open Source, me and many others were called 'communists', just by defending that code and ideas should be shared and made free.

These days there are tons of business models that have been proven to work on top of an Open Source models. For example here are 12 examples[32] :

- Software Support Business Model, Software Services Business Model, Software as a Service (SaaS) Model
- AdWare Business Model
- Consulting Services, Independent Contractors/Developers, Indirect Services & Accessories
- Proprietary Software Model, Premium Software Model, Dual Licensing Model, Hybrid Model, Public Domain Model
- Platform Integration Services, Hardware Integration Model
- Non-Profit Business Models

---

[31]https://www.ece.cmu.edu/~ganger/712.fall02/papers/p761-thompson.pdf
[32]http://www.openhealthnews.com/articles/2012/open-source-business-models-more-depth-view

- Defensive Business Model/Strategy

For Open Source to scale and be sustainable in the long term, it has to be supported by an viable economic model (one where there is a positive feedback loop of value for its creators and maintainers). These examples of Open Source business models (and the successful companies/services that use them) are behind a significant number of the open source contributions that we see today. Of course that there are other forms of receiving value form contributing to Open Source, namely learning something new, contributor brand enhancement or even just purely the joy we get from sharing knowledge.

In a weird way, the Open Source revolution has happened, most of the key battles have been won, but a large number of Gen Z are not aware of it (and are not poised to benefit from these business models and strategies). The danger is that there is still a lot of to do in the Open Source world and we need the Gen Z to be a big driver and innovator.

Releasing code under an Open Source license

Question: 'Why don't you open source your code?'. I bet the answer is a combination of:

- "I don't think my code is good enough"
- "I'm embarrassed about my code"
- "Nobody will want to use my code"

The first thing to understand is that I have heard these same excuses from all sorts of developers and companies, for code in all sorts of quality and completeness.

This is your Lizard brain[33] in action (making excuses of why you shouldn't do something)

The key is to just do it!

Create a GitHub or BitBucket repo, add the license and start building your community.

So how do you Open Source some code?

1. Create a repo and add code to it
2. Add file containing an Open Source license
3. That's it!

And then, after you Open Sourced your app or code, what will happen next is: Nothing!

The reality is that it is very hard to create a community around an open source project (most open source projects have been created and are maintained by a very small number of developers)

What you will have done by adding the license file to your code, is to create future opportunities for that code and sent a strong message about your agenda (i.e. you are not going to lock in the future the users that are using your current code today):

- you are allowing somebody (which could be you) in the future to use your code
- you are also protecting your research, so that if you move companies, you can still use that code (there is nothing worse for a programmer than to having to rewrite something that was working ok (specially when it is a framework that supports a particular workflow)

I believe that we have moral imperative to share our ideas. I don't want to be the one that close ideas and don't let other benefit and

---

[33]https://facilethings.com/blog/en/lizard-brain

learn from them. These days everything you do is a variation of what somebody has done before (i.e. you are adding an incremental change), after all you are sitting in shoulders of the giants that come before you.

Open Source as a way for companies to collaborate and find talent

There has been big success stories of companies collaborating internally externally (i.e. internal collaboration between different teams via open source code)

Ironically, although most developers have internal access to all code, the number of cross-team pull requests is very low. Publishing the same code under an Open Source license will help a lot in its internal reach, usage and collaboration.

This also means that by allowing others to use their code, cleaver companies are creating a great way to find programmers to hire (or companies to buy). As a developer you should take advantage of this and be an active contributor on the open source projects of the companies you want to work for (this is a great way to meet the key developers from those organizations, which might turn up to be key decision makers in your job application)

Open Source as a way to define the agenda

When I see code (or applications) that are not released under an Open Source license, namely the scenarios when the application is provided for 'free; (as in zero cost, not as in freedom), I always think 'What is their agenda?', 'Why are they not Open Sourcing the code?', 'Is this a plan to hook the users, make the dependent on the technology and then start charging at a later stage?'.

When the companies (or authors) release code under an Open Source license they allow their users to have the ability (if they want) to control their own destiny.

Although hard to quantify, I have seen lots of examples where much better engineering decisions have been made due to the fact that ability to lock the user in restrictive licenses is not there.

The Cathedral and the Bazaar

As with many others, my paradigm shift into an Open Source mindset happened 20 years ago after I read the The Cathedral and the Bazaar[34] essay and book, where Eric Raymond provides 19 lessons which are still as relevant today (2018) as when they were published (1998).

Here are some of the best ones:

- Every good work of software starts by scratching a developer's personal itch.
- Good programmers know what to write. Great ones know what to rewrite (and reuse).
- Release early. Release often. And listen to your customers.
- Given a large enough beta-tester and co-developer base, almost every problem will be characterized quickly and the fix obvious to someone.
- If you treat your beta-testers as if they're your most valuable resource, they will respond by becoming your most valuable resource.
- To solve an interesting problem, start by finding a problem that is interesting to you.

In the book Eric compares the creation of proprietary applications to an Cathedral and the development of open source to an Bazaar.

In Eric's view, Cathedrals are: massive and expensive undertakings, take ages to create, don't have much innovation (apart from a couple major areas), have all sorts of top-down management problems,

---

[34]https://en.wikipedia.org/wiki/The_Cathedral_and_the_Bazaar

are super expensive , don't usually work very well (for the intended purposes) and don't usually turn up the way they were originally designed.

On the other hand the Bazaars behave like living organisms, always innovating and with always somebody somewhere trying something new.

I actually prefer to see the beauty in both Cathedrals and Bazaars. Each has it magic and situations when they are exactly what is required.

What I find interesting about this analogy, is that with the understanding that we now have of developing software in ways that are super-effective, that promote continuous refactoring and that are constantly deploying one small/medium change at the time (which is what we get from effective TDD and DevOps environments), we can actually 'build amazing Cathedrals out of Bazaar' (i.e. create an Cathedrals by continuously refactor and improve what started has an Bazaar).

This goes to the heart of what I have noticed in effective development environments with crazy-high code coverage: 'the more code and capabilities are added to the application, the faster changes can be made' (which is the opposite of what happens in a lot of projects, where the higher the quantity of code, the slower everything becomes).

Docker

As a developer it is critical that you understand how Docker works and how it became so successful and widely used. Docker is one of those revolutions that occur regularly in the IT industry where the right product comes at the right time and meets a number of very specific pain points for developers.

From a practical point of view, Docker makes it very easy for you to try and use a wide variety of applications and environments. For example you can start a local (fully working) instance of the ELK Stack[35] (Elastic search + Logstash + Kibana) in Docker, simply by running the sudo Docker pull sebp/elk command (without installing anything on your host machine).

The first time I saw and used Docker, I was massively impressed by its simplicity and its potential to change how applications are developed and deployed.

To understand Docker and its power, the first concept to master is how Docker is a *"process that exposes a multi-layered file system as an fully isolated OS"*

It is easy to see Docker as just a faster VM environment or a faster Vagrant (which is a way to programmatically create VMs). I've seen companies that having automated VM deployments to a significant extent (i.e. they become really good at automating the creation and deployment of multi-gigabyte VMs) completely dismissed Docker as just another IT fad.

The problem is that Docker is much more than just a faster VM and by fast, I mean super-fast. VMs typically take several minutes to fully boot in to a 'ready state'; Docker can give you a fully functional Ubuntu instance with Node installed in sub-second start time (just run Docker run -it node bash and when inside the Docker container run node -e 'console.log(20+22)').

Docker starts in second(s) because it is just a process. The magic sauce is created by:

1. a number of Linux kernel technologies that are able create a sandboxed environment for that process (for files and network access and other key parts of the OS)
2. a layered file system, where each layer contains a diff of the previous layer. This is a powerful graph db, where each file location is dynamically calculated when you are inside the

---

[35]https://www.elastic.co/elk-stack

Docker image. Basically what is happening is that each layer is immutable, and when a file is changed inside Docker it is either a) saved as a new Docker image or b) discarded when the Docker image stops. A final 'Docker image' is just a collection of multiple images, all stacked up, one on top of the other.

Kubernetes

Say you want to:

1. use multiple Docker images in parallel (for example an image for the web server, an image for file system and an image with a database) or
2. Start multiple images at the same time (for example a web server behind a load balancer)

You will need to start looking at what are called 'orchestration technologies'.

The Docker team has published light orchestration frameworks called Docker Compose[36] and Docker Swarm[37]. Whilst both solutions are relatively effective and have their share of pros and cons,Kubernetes[38] is by far the most widely used container orchestration mechanism in production environments.

Kubernetes (sometimes also called K8) was actually developed by Google and was inspired by Google's Borg[39]. The Borg is one of the key reasons why Google was able to massively scale services like its web search and Gmail. Everything at Google is a container and as early as 2014 Google claimed to be starting two billion[40] containers per week[41]

---

[36]https://docs.Docker.com/compose/
[37]https://docs.Docker.com/engine/swarm/
[38]https://en.wikipedia.org/wiki/Kubernetes
[39]https://ai.google/research/pubs/pub43438
[40]https://www.theregister.co.uk/2014/05/23/google_containerization_two_billion/
[41]https://cloud.google.com/containers/

Kubernetes allows the codification of an application environment thus addressing requirements such as deployment strategy, scalability, container hygiene and tracking etc.

This is very powerful, since it allows you to basically say: *"I want x number of pods (i.e. web servers and database) to always be available, and if they stop, make sure they are restarted (and configured accordingly)"*

The reason why it is so important to understand this is because you need to evolve from creating environments by manual 'button clicking' to codifying your service delivery environment (which is just a higher level of programming abstraction layer).

Note that you also get a similar workflow with tools like AWS CloudFormation[42]

One easy way to give Kubernetes a test drive is to use AWS EKS[43]

Security advantages

From a security point of view, Docker has clear advantages.

The first is an explicit mapping of what needs to be installed and what resources (e.g. ports) need to be made available.

Docker also makes it possible to safely run 3rd party code in isolated (i.e. sandboxed) environments, where malicious code running inside a Docker container, would not have access to the current host user's data. This is actually the future of desktop and server-side apps where simple external (or even mission critical) service/code is executed inside containers.

Testing and visualizing Docker

One area where we are still quite immature, as an industry, is the testing of Docker images and Kubernetes setups.

---

[42]https://aws.amazon.com/cloudformation/
[43]https://aws.amazon.com/eks/

There aren't enough good tools, IDEs and Test Runners for Docker and Kubernetes. Basically we need a Test Driven Development (TDD) workflow for Docker development!

If I were you, this would definitely be an area I would focus my research on (while blogging about your efforts).

Another great research area is the visualization and mapping of Kubernetes environments (i.e. who is speaking to who, and how is that traffic authenticated and authorized). See *Weave Scope - Troubleshooting & Monitoring for Docker & Kubernetes*[44] for an interesting Open Source project in this space.

You would have a big competitive advantage in the market place if you understood these concepts and had practical experience at implementing them.

It all stated with physical containers

For a great introduction to Containers see MAYA Design's Containerization[45] animation, and the Wendover Productions' Containerization: The Most Influential Invention That You've Never Heard Of[46] video

To see what is coming next see MAYA Design's Trillions[47] - video and the Trillions: Thriving in the Emerging Information Ecology[48] book

Jira

Jira[49] is a web application that is widely used by development,

---

[44]https://github.com/weaveworks/scope
[45]https://vimeo.com/49392667
[46]https://www.youtube.com/watch?v=F-ZskaqBshs
[47]https://vimeo.com/7395079
[48]https://www.amazon.co.uk/Trillions-Thriving-Emerging-Information-Ecology/dp/1118176073
[49]https://www.atlassian.com/software/jira

engineering and technical teams to manage their day to day tasks and activities.

There is massive worldwide adoption by all types of companies, and we (at Photobox Group Security) use Jira extensively in our day-to-day. We use it for example to manage: vulnerabilities, risks, task management, incident handling, OKRs management, asset register, threat modeling, data journeys and even to create an pseudo org chart for the stakeholders of risks.

To make this work we are very advanced users of Jira, where we create tons of custom Workflows and even write custom applications that consume Jira's APIs.

We basically use Jira as an graph database and Confluence[50] as a way to display the information stored in JIRA. See the Creating a Graph Based Security Organization[51] presentation for more ideas on how we do this.

The key point I want to make here is: in order to make the tools that we use in the enterprise work, they need to be customized and extended.

Being able to write these customization's and understanding at a much deeper level what is possible with these tools, when compared to 'normal' or 'power' users, is a massive competitive advantage. Customizing and extending tools should not be seen as an exception, it should be the rule.

The reason this scales is due to the compound effect (i.e. increased returns) of the features implemented. The changes/features we make today, will make us more productive tomorrow, which will help us to make more changes, which make us even more productive.

In fact as a developer, if you are able to write custom JIRA workflows that are usable by your team, that will be another competitive

---

[50]https://www.atlassian.com/software/confluence
[51]https://www.slideshare.net/DinisCruz/creating-a-graph-based-security-organisation-devseccon-keynote-81345667

advantage for you, and it will make you highly employable today.

Reality is the complex one

It is important to note that once the complexities and interconnections of reality start to be mapped in Jira, it can be very overwhelming.

For example we use Jira heavily in our incident handling process, where we can easily create 100+ issues during an incident, with each issue being a relevant question or action to be answers or executed during the incident. It is easy to look at that setup and think that it is too complex and a massive bureaucracy. But in reality that combination of issues (of type: Incident, Task, Vulnerability and Epics) is an accurate representation of the complex reality and massive amount of information that is created during an incident. The alternative are completely unmanageable and unreadable email, slack threads or word docs).

All the work comes together via powerful up-to-date Confluence pages (which we convert to PDFs and distribute via slack/email) to answer the key questions of: 'What has happened?', 'What are the facts?', 'What are the hypothesis we are exploring?', 'What is happening now?' and 'What are the next steps?'. This is how we keep everybody involved in sync, and how we provide regular management updates.

The other big advantage of this setup is that it allows us to do very effective post-incident analysis and to create playbooks with predefined tasks to be executed when a similar incident occurs in the future. Basically our playbooks are not a word document with tasks and actions, our playbooks are a lists of Jira Tasks that are used to populate the incident set of tasks.

For more ideas about this topic see the SecDevOps Risk Workflow[52] book that I'm also writing and the SecDevOps Risk Workflow -

---

[52]https://leanpub.com/secdevops/

v0.6[53] presentation .

Use Jira in your life

Create Jira projects for your life activities, with Epics to track group of tasks.

Create a Kanban board for your personal tasks and Epics.

Create custom workflows and learn how to manage Jira. This will give you tons of confidence when using Jira in the real world or when intervening.

And since Atlassian has evaluation version for their cloud version of Jira, there isn't any cost to try this. You have no excuse for not using Jira before, at a level more advanced that most corporate users and the developers interviewing you.

What makes Jira so powerful

Although Jira has tons of really annoying features and bugs, its feature set is very powerful. With finely tunned process and customization's it will make the difference on your productivity and will change how you work.

Here are some of Jira's really powerful features:

- **Issues** - that can be easily linked to each other (i.e. nodes and edges)
- **Links** - which can be named, and allow the creation of named edges, for example 'RISK-111 is-created-by VULN-222'
- **Workflows** - state machine environment where the issue's status can be visually mapped and powerful buttons be created, for example for status transitions like 'Accept Risk'

---

[53]https://www.slideshare.net/DinisCruz/secdevops-risk-workflow-v06

- **Activity logging** - ability to log every change and status transition
- **Labels** - ability to apply all sorts of loosely created labels/tags to issues (we use this to help managing specific workflows, for example by adding the 'Needs_Risk_Mapping' label to an issue)
- **Components** - ability to map issues to components which map directly into business' areas or applications
- **Kanban boards** - powerful way to view the current tasks and what status they are
- **Dashboards** - ability to create all sorts of diagrams and tables from Jira data (although we tend to use Confluence for data visualization)

Its all about People, Process and Technology

In order to create a successful Jira environment, the 'Technology' part, we have to start with the 'People' part (in this case you). It is the mindset of the individual user that helps to kickstart these workflows.

The 'Process' of how things work is the other key element. I found it's very hard for participants to really 'get' these processes and to really understand at a deeper level how the hyperlinked graph-based architecture works. By nature there will be a lot of changes, not only of past workflows, but of existing workflows. Change is the only constant.

Ironically this means that Jira is not key to make this work.

I have built similar systems using GitHub.

Although GitHub doesn't have some of the most advanced features of Jira (like workflows), the fact that GitHub has native Markdown support, that all content is managed using git and that it is super fast, makes it also an effective graph database.

With the right People and Process, lots of Technologies can be used to make this work. As long as they can be used a Graph Database with every piece of data being available in an hyperlinkable way

OWASP

OWASP[54] (the Open Web Application Security Project) is a worldwide organization focused on Application Security. We are the good guys that are trying to make the world a safer place :)

I have been heavily involved in OWASP for a long time, and it is one of the more open, friendly, knowledgeable and carer-enhancing communities you can find. I've meet some of my best friends in the industry though OWASP and what I've learned from its projects and events is too long to list here :)

There are many ways that actively participating in OWASP will make you a better developer and enhance your carer. Part of building your brand, skills and network is the participation in Open Source communities, and OWASP is a a perfect place to do that.

The first place to start is your local Owasp Chapter. With 100s of chapters[55] worldwide, you shouldn't be to far from one (if not then start one[56], the London Chapter started many years ago over beers in a London pub). Attend a chapter meeting, learn something new and create connections.

Next step is to check out the OWASP projects[57] and see which ones are relevant to your current work/research, and more importantly, which ones you should be involved as a contributor. Most OWASP projects, even the bigger and most successful ones, are usually maintained by only a couple individuals, and ALL projects are desperate for contributors and help! It is not that hard to start, just

---

[54]https://www.owasp.org/

[55]https://www.owasp.org/index.php/OWASP_Chapter

[56]https://www.tfaforms.com/261541

[57]https://www.owasp.org/index.php/Category:OWASP_Project#tab=Project_Inventory

fork the project in GitHub, see the open issues and start sending the Pull Requests.

Check out the main OWASP Conferences[58] and events like the Open Security Summit[59] which are amazing places to learn and meet highly talented professionals, all happy to share knowledge and teach.

Finally, join up OWASP Slack[60] where you will find everybody and 100s of channels dedicated to everything OWASP related (projects, chapters, conferences, topics)

Find jobs via OWASP contributions

Due to its open nature and focus on finding solutions for hard problems (related to application security), OWASP's community is made by the 'doers', i.e. the ones that actually get things done at companies and know what they are doing.

This means that regardless if you want to want to get a job in an security team, active participation in OWASP projects is a perfect and very effective way to meet individuals that can help you find the job you want.

That said, there is a massive skills shortage in the market for Application Security specialists. The main reason is because you can't really do Application Security unless you have a developer background. My advise to all developers I meet, is to seriously consider an Application Security carer. Not only it is an industry that is on a massive growth curve, it really needs new talent, energy , development skill and ideas.

---

[58]https://www.owasp.org/index.php/Category:OWASP_AppSec_Conference
[59]https://open-security-summit.org/
[60]http://owaspslack.com

Python

Python[61] is great language to master since it contains a large number of the key development paradigms that you need to know, while being easy to learn and read.

Python started in 1991 by Guido van Rossum[62] when he was 35 and the key focus was in making a simple but powerful language.

A great feature added early on was the REPL (Read Eval Print Loop) environment. This is what you see when you run `python` from the command line and get an interactive shell that allows the execution of Python code. That said, I don't use the Python command line very often, since I have a similar (and more powerful) REPL environment using Python tests (and TDD)

Use Python for AWS automation

Even if you are not using Python as your main development language, due to it massive adoption and powerful ability to write small apps/function, you should use it often (for all sorts of automation tasks).

A perfect example of the power of Python is in the development of Serverless functions (executed as an AWS Lambda function[63]) or in advanced customization's of event-driven workflows (like the one provided by Zapier Python support[64])

The AWS SDK for python (boto3)[65] is something you should spend quite a lot of time with and really explore its capabilities (while learning to take python into another level).

---

[61]https://en.wikipedia.org/wiki/Python_(programming_language)

[62]https://twitter.com/gvanrossum/

[63]https://docs.aws.amazon.com/lambda/latest/dg/python-programming-model-handler-types.html

[64]https://zapier.com/help/code-python/

[65]https://boto3.amazonaws.com/v1/documentation/api/latest/index.html

This API gives you access to just about everything you can do in AWS, and as a developer you need to really start thinking of AWS as an 'app' that you code your application on top of its capabilities. You need to get into the practice of writing code (driven by tests) vs clicking on things.

For example here is a code snippet that starts a virtual machine in AWS:

```
1  import boto3
2  ec2         = boto3.client('ec2')
3  instance_id = sys.argv[2]
4  response    = ec2.start_instances(InstanceIds=[inst\
5  ance_id])
6  print(response)
```

Don't click on things

Clicking on an UI with your mouse, is a non-repeatable, non-automated and non-scalable way to perform a specific task. What you want to do is to write tools, APIs and DSLs that allow the easy and automated execution of those tasks.

For example here is a python script that tests the execution of an Lambda function

```
 1       def test_hello_world(self):
 2           handler        = 'lambdas.s3.hello_world.r\
 3   un'
 4           payload        = {"name": "lambda-runner"}
 5           expected_result = 'hello {0}'.format(payloa\
 6   d.get('name'))
 7
 8           self.aws.lambda_create_function(self.name, \
 9   self.role, handler, self.s3_bucket, self.s3_key)
10           result = self.aws.lambda_invoke_function(se\
11   lf.name, payload)
12           assert result == expected_result
```

Python for data parsing and analysis

Another really powerful use of Python is to perform all sorts of data parsing, modeling and analysis.

As a very practical real world scenario, if somebody sends me multiple excel documents with data to analyse, the first thing I do is to:

- export it to csv,
- use python to normalize the raw data into json file(s)
- use an data visualizing tool or API (for example ELK, Neo4J or visjs[66]).

This is not very hard to do, and is faster then trying to make sense of the excel documents (namely when needing to do data correlation between different excel sheets or files)

---

[66]http://visjs.org/

Slack and ChatOps

It is easy to underestimate Slack[67]'s capabilities, not realise that Slack is a massive agent for change, and that Slack's empowered workflows will play a big part in your future as a developer.

Initially Slack might look like just an evolution of instant messaging tools like: Skype[68], MSN Messenger[69], SMS[70], ICQ[71], IRC[72] or Smoke Signals[73].

The reason why Slack in a relative short period (5 years) gained such adoption and traction, is because its features enable organizations and communities to not only to change how they communicate, but how they behave. Namely how they understand what is going on and how they respond to events.

Effective Communication and alignment are not only key competitive advantages of successful organizations, but are usually the reason they succeed or fail (see "Aligning vectors"[74] presentation for more details).

Slack provides an Asynchronous data/information exchange environment that can be at the epicenter of the multiple actors involved in the organization ecosystem: humans, bots, servers, applications, services and events.

The potential for change is enormous, although at the moment, most companies are only taking advantage of about 10% of Slack's capabilities. In most organizations Slack is at the *'replacing email'* stage, which quickly is followed by the *'too many channels'* and

---

[67]https://slack.com/
[68]https://en.wikipedia.org/wiki/Skype
[69]https://en.wikipedia.org/wiki/Windows_Live_Messenger
[70]https://en.wikipedia.org/wiki/SMS
[71]https://en.wikipedia.org/wiki/ICQ
[72]https://en.wikipedia.org/wiki/Internet_Relay_Chat
[73]https://en.wikipedia.org/wiki/Smoke_signal
[74]https://www.linkedin.com/pulse/what-elon-musk-taught-me-growing-business-dharmesh-shah/

'how do find what is going on without having to read a gigantic slack thread' phases (which can have diminishing returns)

The important question for you is: *"Are you going to take an active and proactive role in making Slack work for an organization?"*. I can guarantee you that if you have hands on experience in the ideas and techniques described in this chapter, you have just increased your competitive advantage and employability.

Why was Slack successful?

Slack's success is a great case study of the power of marginal gains, where a large number of 1% improvements created an spectacular platform (for another great example 1% marginal gains the see the British' cycle success on *How 1% Performance Improvements Led to Olympic Gold*[5] where they talk about the power of marginal gains, based on 3 areas: strategy, human performance and continuous improvement).

Here are some of the features that Slack added that (in aggregation) made a massive difference:

- **Copy and Paste of images** - this 'simple' feature massively improves the user's workflow and ability to communicate (It still amazes me how companies don't realise that there is a massive usability difference between copy and pasting an image and having to upload an image). If I remember correctly this was one of the reasons I started to like Slack
- **Effective use of Emojis** - not only for emotions (happy/sad/angry/laughing face) but for actions/decisions (yes/no, ok, 'read document', 'need more details')
- **Great desktop application** - with seamless integration with web and mobile (the desktop app is built of top of Electron[76])
- **Effective search and shortcuts**

---

[75]https://hbr.org/2015/10/how-1-performance-improvements-led-to-olympic-gold
[76]https://electronjs.org/

- **Drag and drop of documents** - with ability to preview them in slack (for example pdfs)
- **Auto previews of links dropped** - like web pages, twitter links, videos
- **Buttons and forms to drive actions** - which allow the expansion/improvement of Slack's UI by 3rd party apps/services
- **3rd party integrations** and **Native support for Bots**
- **Smooth and regular deployment of new features** (audio and voice conferencing, single channel users, message reminders, message threads). Here is an example of a *Same day fix*[77] which highlights the power of DevOps and Continuous Deployment
- **Scalable backend with very few outages**
- **Application Security** and **Security usability**
- **Great culture and focus** - see the *Dear Microsoft*[78] Ad they run in Nov 2016 and the internal memo from July 2013 *We Don't Sell Saddles Here*[79]

All of the above combined (can) create a super productive environment. Your task is to be a 'Slack master' and lead the revolution :)

The big lesson here is that:

1. high focus on where you add value, speed of delivery and adaptability of the direction of travel

beats

1. a highly defined strategy

---

[77]https://twitter.com/p0cket/status/784141207601614848
[78]https://slackhq.com/dear-microsoft
[79]https://medium.com/@stewart/we-dont-sell-saddles-here-4c59524d650d

For a great example of changing directions, if you check out Slack's history[80] you will see that Slack actually started as an internal tool created by the company *Tiny Speck* while they were working on the Glitch[81] game

Learn how to use Slack

As with every tool, you need to spend time in learning how to use it in order to be effective. It is very important to initially not be overwhelmed by the large number of channels and messages that you will get.

Fun fact, when things get quite heavy, sometimes we call it *'Slack Tennis'* since there is so much stuff bouncing around in multiple channels that it fells like you are playing Tennis inside Slack.

Some practical tips:

- remove most Slack notifications
- mute chatty channels that don't provide important information for your day to day activities
- do to not be afraid to leave a channel, since if you are needed, it is easy for others to bring you in with a mention of your name
- consume Slack under your terms, not when a message arrives and you receive a dopamine kick

Think of Slack as asynchronous communications, where there is a gap of time between when:

1. a message is sent
2. a message is received
3. a message is processed (with our without a reply)

---

[80]https://en.wikipedia.org/wiki/Slack_(software)
[81]https://en.wikipedia.org/wiki/Glitch_(video_game)

As with just about everything, the challenges are one of People, Process and Technology:

- **People** - you and and who/what you are communicating with
- **Process** - how Slack is used (conversions, workflows, human behaviors, response's protocols/expectations, new users on-boarding, documentation)
- **Technology** - Slack and its integrations

The good news is that you have direct control over these three, and there is nothing stopping you from learning.

This is why your understanding and use of Slack is a major sign of your own values and skills.

There is no cost in learning and using slack in the ways I describe in this chapter.

If you don't learn how to effectively use Slack, what is that telling about your drive, priorities, energy, desire to learn and ability to effectively use new technologies. Basically your competitive advantages in the marketplace is directly related to how you use Slack.

ChatOps

Let's go up a gear and start looking at what makes Slack so powerful. I'm talking about Bot Integration.

Bots are basically applications (ideally setup in a serverless pipeline) that react or generate events. For example we could have a bot that:

1. receives a notification from an live server (an CPU Spike, new deployment, or an particular user action) or from an 3rd party service (like email, twitter or CI pipeline)
2. processes and (optionally) transforms it

3. sends a follow-up slack message to a particular channel (based on a pre-defined set of rules)
4. gets response from user (simple acknowledgement or action)
5. reacts to that response

The concept that clearly explains this workflow is the '*ChatOps*' idea, which was initially shared in the amazing 'Chatops At GitHub'[82] presentation (see video here[83]). For more recent presentations see Real World ChatOps[84], Revolutionize Your Workflow with ChatOps[85] and Accelerating DevOps with ChatOps[86]

One of the definitions of ChatOps is "*a collaboration model that connects people, tools, process, and automation into a transparent workflow*" that creates a *Culture of Automation, Measurement and Sharing* (CAMS). This basically means that ChatOps is at the epicenter of information and decisions flows.

A real world example is when you (as a developer) use Slack as a communication medium for what is going on (in your live servers, test's execution or even build). But even more interesting, not only you can get data into Slack, you can issue back commands and influence what is going on.

Getting started

The best way to learn is by doing it.

Your first step is to create a Slack workspace[87] so that you have a playground for your ideas. There is no cost[88] to create new Slack Workspace, so what are you waiting for?

---

[82]https://speakerdeck.com/jnewland/chatops-at-github
[83]https://www.youtube.com/watch?v=NST3u-GjjFw
[84]https://www.slideshare.net/VictorOps/real-world-chatops
[85]https://www.slideshare.net/Tessa99/revolutionize-your-workflow-with-chatops
[86]https://www.slideshare.net/rohanrath/accelerating-devops-with-chatops-91945690
[87]https://slack.com/create
[88]https://slack.com/pricing

Make sure you invite your friends and colleagues to participate, so that you have a wide set of scenarios to play with.

To get you going here are a couple scenarios:

- write code that sends messages to a slack channel (simple HTTP POST requests with your Slack API key)
- follow GitHub's footsteps and deploy and customize Hubot[89]. Errbot[90] is a Python alternative, and Slack's tutorial shows an integration using Botkit[91]
- write bot integrations with services like Zapier[92] or IFTTT[93]. See Zapier's *How to Build Your Own Slack Bot in 5 minutes*[94] guide
- write a serverless Slack integration using AWS API Gateway and Lambda functions
- write a Slack integration that automates one area of your life (maybe something to do with a task you do every day)

Join the OWASP Slack Community

OWASP (Open Web Application Security Project) is an very friendly open source community that has migrated a large part of its digital interactions to Slack (see OWASP chapter[95] for more details).

I strongly advise you to join the Owasp Slack using this registration form[96].

Not only you will see examples of these integrations in real-world scenarios, in that workspace you will find a multiple Slack experts,

---

[89]https://hubot.github.com/
[90]http://errbot.io/
[91]https://api.slack.com/tutorials/easy-peasy-bots
[92]https://zapier.com/
[93]https://ifttt.com/
[94]https://zapier.com/blog/how-to-build-chat-bot/
[95]https://github.com/DinisCruz/Book_Generation_Z_Developer/blob/master/content/2. mvp-for-gen-z-dev/content/owasp.md
[96]http://owaspslack.com

who will be more than happy to help you. You can also find multiple opportunities (in OWASP project or chapters) to put your Slack integration skills in action.

When you join in, drop me a message saying Hi. I should be easy to find :)

Talking to yourself via Slack

As I mention in the Talking to yourself digitally[97] chapter, the practice of capturing your thoughts and workflows is super important.

Slack is a great medium to do this, since it massively improves the workflow that we we usually have when using Word docs (or services like Evernote[98]) to capture notes about what we are doing.

Here is the workflow I usually use:

1. in Slack describe what I am going to try next
2. do it
3. take screenshot of the latest change
4. in Slack paste the screenshot
5. go back to 1.

This workflow is really powerful, because what you are doing is capturing how you are thinking about the problem you are solving (including all the tangents that you tried and didn't work). And yes, very often, you will find that it is only you that (initially): asks questions, provides answers, learn from failures and celebrates successes.

One way to keep sanity is to remember that this information will be super useful one day to your *future self*, and that you now have the raw data / screenshots for a great blog post. This will help

---

[97]https://github.com/DinisCruz/Book_Generation_Z_Developer/blob/master/content/4.
life-patterns/content/talking-to-yourself.md
[98]https://evernote.com/

others to understand the steps you took, the challenges you had, the solutions that didn't work, the solutions that did work, and how to arrived at the final result/conclusion.

This is also how you scale your knowledge and avoid having to answer the same question twice (specially when you create a blog post which makes it really easy to find that content)

A simpler version of this pattern is when you:

1. ask a question in Slack
2. find the answer
3. reply to your own message with the solution

Use Slack when debugging code (as a log collector)

When you have a bug in your code that you don't understand the root cause, a common practice is to use a Debugger[99], which will provide features like breakpoints and code stepping.

This just about works when you have direct access to the execution environment and you are looking at simple applications.

But as soon as you start working on distributed systems with lots of moving parts (for example with multiple web services and serverless functions), you stop having the ability to really understand what is going on (namely the exact sequence of events and what the data looks like in those intermediate states)

Slack gives you an environment to receive logs/messages from those internal execution flow and states. To make this scale, you should create helper APIs that make it easy to send and receive data from Slack.

As simple example, here is a Python method that I wrote to help me understand and debug AWS Lambda function's execution:

---

[99]https://en.wikipedia.org/wiki/Debugger

```
1   send_to_slack('there are {0} missing ips'.format(le\
2   n(missing)))
3
4       ...(do something)...
5
6   send_to_slack('resolving {0} missing ips'.format(le\
7   n(missing)))
8
9       ...(do something)...
10
11  send_to_slack('resolved {0} ipdata ips'.format(len(\
12  ipdatas)))
```

Hugo

Hugo IO[100] is a SWG (Static Website Generator that represents a very interesting twist on the development stack of a website (another popular Static Website Generator is Jekyll[101])

In addition to having a great environment to create content (and to maintain it), what hugo creates is a completely different paradigm shift on how to create and publish websites.

Basically an SWG pre-generates all possible web pages during the build stage .... and that's it!

Once the build is finished (usually in less than a second), the entire content of the website is available in an local/CI folder, that can be easily deployed/copied/synced with any server or service that is able to host static files (for example AWS S3[102])

In practice this means that you have a website running from vanilla web pages, with no backed and no moving parts. Not only this is

---

[100]https://gohugo.io
[101]https://jekyllrb.com/
[102]https://aws.amazon.com/s3

massively secure (no server-side code to hack), this has amazing performance implications (i.e. the site is super fast, when compared with dynamically generated sites).

"Why no backend?" Well ... ask yourself the question: "Why do you need a database?" (i.e. What is the database actually doing, that you can't pre-generated all in one go?)

It is amazing how in any real-world scenarios a database is not actually needed!

That said, Hugo is actually using a very efficient and scalable database and cache: The file system :)

I really like the pattern of using the file system as a database, specially when combined with git for deployment, and GitHub for CMS (Content Management System)

Hugo also makes it really easy to create (and understand) an CD (Continuous Deployment) environment. Since it covers the key steps required:

- build the site
- edit the site
- see changes
- publish/sync the generated files (to a server/service serving static files)
- (ideally you should also be writing tests, which I would do using: NodeJS, CoffeeScript, Mocha, Cheerio and WallabyJS)

Another key feature is the integration with LiveReload[103] (which very important to experience in a practical/personal way). Assuming you have the editor and web browser side-by-side in your screen, Hugo+LiveReload creates an environment where you can see your content changes immediately reflected in the browser, in

---

[103]https://github.com/livereload/livereload-js

an quasi-real-time way (i.e as soon as the file is saved, the browser is reloaded and the new content in rendered)

Hugo is also a great case-study of how modern development techniques, technologies, and open source innovation create products/apis that are miles ahead of the competition, with killer features.

After using and developing all sorts of CMS (Content Management Systems), I have to say that it gives me a spectacular and highly-productive content creation/editing workflow.

I use Hugo a lot these days, in all sort of internal and external sites, here are some examples:

- The Open Security Summit 2018 website (https://open-security-summit.org/) is a highly complex data driven website (which will look like a database-powered site) that is entirely built on top of Hugo. All source code is available on this GitHub repo[104] and the Hugo setup enabled 157 contributors to create 3575 commits
- The Photobox Group Security Site (https://pbx-group-security.com/) is a simpler example of a fully working Hugo site in action
- This book you are reading uses Hugo in two ways: 1) locally hosted website with a number of extra pages that helps to improve my productivity when writing the book (for example: an hugo-based search, and print-friendly pages), 2) markdown generation for Leanpub publishing (which adds a couple extra features like the ability to create the MVP table from the content of its child pages)

Simple example (MVP)

Here is simple example of my very first test of using Hugo where changes on the left are shown automagically on the right. I always

---

[104]https://github.com/OpenSecuritySummit/oss2018

start learning a new technology by creating the simplest possible version that works, i.e. an MVP.

More advanced example (with graphs)

Here is a more advanced usage of Hugo, where we are using Hugo to create VisJs visualizations of Neo4J graphs populated from JIRA data

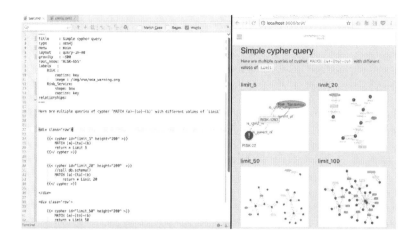

Do Static Site Generators scale?

Although I prefer Hugo to Jekyll, here are two amazing examples of using Jekyll at scale:

- HealthCare.gov - see *It's Called Jekyll, and It Works*[105]
- Obama's fundraising website - see *Meet the Obama campaign's $250 million fundraising platform*[106]

Google Search, GDD and SRE

As a developer one of the most important skills you need to learn is how to GDD.

GDD stands for is Google Driven Development, and it is how every professional developer codes these days. Google's search engine is so powerful and effective that when coding (and learning), Google's Search Engine can point to the correct answers much better than anyone or anything else.

---

[105]https://developmentseed.org/blog/2013/10/24/its-called-jekyll/
[106]http://kylerush.net/blog/meet-the-obama-campaigns-250-million-fundraising-platform/

Why is Google Search so good?

Google's search magic is created by the WebGraph[107] inspired PageRank[108] algorithm, which decides the order of the search results. One of the first major innovations of this algorithm was the use of a number of links to point to particular page as an indicator of the page relevance. The other major innovation was the feedback loop between what the users are clicking and the position of the link in the page. This means that every time you click on a link in Google, you are voting with your answer and teaching Google's PageRank algorithm. To see this in action, notice when you copy the link of a Google Search result, the link is not to the page you want to see. The link is to a google service that will capture and store your choice. It is the capture of this data that allows Google to benefit from network effects[109] and provide custom search results to each user. Yes, when you search for a particular topic you will get different results from somebody else.

Here is a challenge for you: *"how can you prove that google shows different results for different users and in different geographical locations?"*. To answer this question effectively, in fact based way, you need to programmatically detect changes in google's behavior. To do this, write using a Cloud environment, an api /tool or set of serverless functions that: - is able to use Google.com to search for results from multiple IPs and geographical regions (in an pure anonymous way, and in ways that Google search engine can track each one of you 'test users') - captures the responses, namely the order of the link's titles (my preference is to use services like S3 as a data store, for the raw data and any transformations done into JSON files) - visualizes and compare the results (my preference is to use ELK and Neo4J as visualization and analysis engines) - presents the data in easy to consume ways (my preference is to use Hugo to create a site that allows the easy navigation of the 'story you want

---

[107]https://en.wikipedia.org/wiki/Webgraph
[108]https://en.wikipedia.org/wiki/PageRank
[109]https://en.wikipedia.org/wiki/Network_effect

to tell')

Also very interesting is the evolution[110] of Google's Search technology into an Knowledge Graph (which has been happening since 2010[111]). The real power in Google's search engine is the gigantic and hyperlinked graph (powered by machine learning) that is able to understand the meaning and intent of the queries made.

For Google Search, you are the product

The clever part of Google Search business model is their turning of the product (i.e. the users doing the searches) into actual 'workers' for Google. Remember that for Google, you are not the client. Google's primary focus and center of gravity is not you.

Google Adwords[112] is the system that allows everybody to buy (and bid for) the placement of Ads on a particular Google search keyword. Adwords is by far the highest income stream for Google, with $94 Billion in revenue in 2017. A key problem with Ad based services that are 'free' but generate billions for the owners of the network, is the reality that you (the user) are the product. You are the 'goods' that Google sells to their real customers (the companies buying the ads).

This is why Google's business model is at odds with privacy. From Google's (and Facebook, Twitter, LinkedIn, etc..) point of view, the less Privacy you have, the more they know about you, the more a valuable asset you become (an asset that they will sell to the highest bidder).

My view is that this business model is reaching its peak and two major changes will happen in this space in the short to medium term. The move to make the user the real customer and the move to reward the users that add value to networks:

---

[110]https://medium.com/s/story/what-google-teaches-us-2613711712de
[111]https://mashable.com/2012/02/13/google-knowledge-graph-change-search/
[112]https://en.wikipedia.org/wiki/AdWords

1. Once the balance shifts back to the user and the protection of user data (with Privacy elevated to a Human right and something companies want to provide for their employees), the protection and anonymization of user's data will be an area with massive growth. And in ways that make the process of sharing and using personal data more secure, efficient and even more profitable.

2. Jaron Lanier in *You are not a Gadget*[113] defends the idea that creators of digital value should be paid for their contributions (in micro-payments). If you look at the income of Google and other community/Ad driven companies, you can see that the rewards and financial returns for the value created by the product (i.e. the users) is today very one sided (with small exception for areas like YouTubers[114] and Medium Writers[115]).

You would be very wise to spend time researching and learning about these paradigm shifts, namely how it will impact development practices and the code that you write.

Do know how to use Google's Search Engine?

How much do you really know about how to search Google for text (images, ideas, videos, books) in the most efficient and effective way?

Have you spent time to learn how to search using Google[116]? Google is just another tool, and you need to spend time learning how to use it and become a master at how to access and query the wealth of information that it stores.

---

[113]https://www.amazon.co.uk/You-Are-Not-Gadget-Manifesto/dp/0141049111

[114]https://en.wikipedia.org/wiki/YouTuber

[115]https://medium.com/words-for-life/a-100-transparent-look-at-my-first-medium-paycheck-197b69483b44

[116]https://support.google.com/websearch/answer/134479?hl=en&ref_topic=3081620

A great place to start is the Advanced Search[117] page and this great list of Google Search Operators[118].

Once you've done that, take a look at Google Dorks[119] which is a Google Hacking technique that searches for sensitive data exposed by Google's Crawlers. To get an idea of what is possible check out the Google Hacking Database[120] which has sections like: Sensitive Directories, Files Containing Passwords, Sensitive Online Shopping Info , Network or Vulnerability Data and much more. You will be surprised, amazed and horrified with what you will discover.

I always find that the best way to learn a technology is using the techniques and patterns used to exploit it; because security tends to go deeper into what is 'really possible', not just how it is 'supposed to be used'. In this case, the Google Hacking Database will give you tons of examples of WTF!, how is this data exposed to the internet? More interesting and relevant to your quest into becoming a better developer, this data will make you ask the questions: *'How did that search query work?'* and *'How did Google Crawlers found that data?'* (which is the best way to learn)

Google's history and scale

Google is one of the best Software engineering companies in the world, and one of the first companies to do *'Internet Scale'* really well.

Google is also massive in open source with highly successful hundreds of projects[121] projects like Angular JS, Android or Kubernetes. Google hires some of the best Open Source developers to work on internal projects related to their passion, for example Guido van Rossum[122] who is Python's founder and lead developer, worked at

---

[117]https://www.google.com/advanced_search
[118]https://ahrefs.com/blog/google-advanced-search-operators/
[119]https://en.wikipedia.org/wiki/Google_hacking
[120]https://www.exploit-db.com/google-hacking-database/
[121]https://opensource.google.com/
[122]https://en.wikipedia.org/wiki/Guido_van_Rossum

Google. By the way, being hired to work on Open Source projects is a very common practice by companies that actively use a particular technology or language. This is a great way to get a dream job: write an Open Source tool/package and get hired by a company that uses it.

Google's profits from the Search Engine are so high that it was able to fund a large number ideas and industries. It got so big that in 2015 the founders of Google created the Alphabet[123] parent company. This is a really cleaver move since it will make each division (from self-driving cars, to drone deliveries) more accountable and focused.

Learn from Google's focus on engineering and SRE

Part of the reason Google has gained massive amounts of market share is due to its ability to experiment and then execute at Scale. Google allows employees to spend 20% of their time on ideas they are passionate about, which sounds crazy at first, but there is solid data[124] that says that this practice is highly effective and that it empowers developers to create new products and services. For example Google services like AdSense, Gmail, Google Maps, Google News or Google Talk where initially developed under the 20% research time.

Google also has a very high bar for quality and engineering. Two good books that explore their practices is the How Google Tests Software[125] and the Site Reliability Engineering[126].

The SRE (Site Reliability Engineering)[127] is an amazing concept, that you as a developer really need to spend time learning and under-

---

[123]https://en.wikipedia.org/wiki/Alphabet_Inc.

[124]https://www.inc.com/bryan-adams/12-ways-to-encourage-more-free-thinking-and-innovation-into-any-business.html

[125]https://www.amazon.co.uk/Google-Tests-Software-James-Whittaker/dp/0321803027

[126]https://www.amazon.co.uk/Site-Reliability-Engineering-Betsy-Beyer/dp/149192912X

[127]https://landing.google.com/sre/

standing how it works (especially how SREs behave). At Google, the SRE teams are the ones that deploy and maintain applications. There are many lessons that we can learn from Google's experience of deploying things at scale. For example I really like the SRE idea to spend 50% on 'doing X' and 50% in improving the process + tools required to effective do that 'X'. 'Error Budgets'[128] are another SRE concept which can make a massive difference in how applications are developed and tested. The SRE idea of 'Error Budget' is that each application or service needs to provides a clear and objective metric of how unreliable that service is allowed to be within a single period of time.

Google also puts a lot of effort in understanding from a scientific point of view, and how to create great teams. See 'Work Rules'[129] book, *Not A Happy Accident: How Google Deliberately Designs Workplace Satisfaction*[130] and Why Google defined a new discipline to help humans make decisions[131] (which introduces the role of *Chief Decision Officer* and the field of *Decision Intelligence Engineering*)

Xcode and Swift

If don't have a Mac computer you can ignore this chapter (or use MacinCloud[132] to rent one).

With a Mac there is nothing stopping you from being hours away from your first Mac or iPhone application.

Xcode[133] is Apple's main development environment, and you can

---

[128]https://landing.google.com/sre/book/chapters/embracing-risk.html

[129]https://www.amazon.co.uk/Work-Rules-Insights-Inside-Transform-ebook/dp/B00NLHJKBE

[130]https://www.fastcompany.com/3007268/not-happy-accident-how-google-deliberately-designs-workplace-satisfaction

[131]https://www.fastcompany.com/90203073/why-google-defined-a-new-discipline-to-help-humans-make-decisions

[132]https://www.macincloud.com

[133]https://en.wikipedia.org/wiki/Xcode

download it for free from the Apple store. Xcode contains everything you need you develop an Mac or iPhone application, namely an IDE, an Debugger and an execution Simulator (iOS, iPad and MacBooks)

Swift[134] is the modern Open Source language developed by Apple that I highly recommend that you use. Swift dramatically simplifies the creation of applications for macOS, iOS, watchOS and tvOS.

Creating your own application is a major milestone in your programming career. You should do it even if you don't want to become an mobile developer. Not only you will learn a large number of key concepts, you will also gain an understanding of how relatively easy it is to go from an idea in your head into a deployed application.

First application

To kickstart your development and experiments, start with step-by-step tutorials like the *Hello World! Build Your First App in Swift*[135] which will guide you through the code and technologies required to make it happen.

After building your first application, your next objective is to think of an use-case that will help you to do something better in your life. This is an **App for you** and the only thing that matters is that it is useful enough that you use it regularly.

One of the key reasons why it is important at this stage that this application is only used by you (or a couple of your friends) is because that way, you can use the Xcode simulators to execute it (i.e. you don't have to release it to the AppStore).

By using the application everyday, you will get direct feedback from what works, what doesn't what and what need improvement. Initially, try to release a new version at least once a week (or once

---

[134]https://developer.apple.com/swift/
[135]https://www.appcoda.com/learnswift/build-your-first-app.html

a day). It is important to create a process for this release (ideally with as much automation as possible).

Make sure you release your application under an Open Source license like Apache 2.0 and that you share it on a GitHub repository. This will allow you to expand your user base and gain more users.

Write tests and create a CI pipeline

Other key workflows that you need to adopt is writing tests and executing them in a CI (Continuous Integration) environment.

See Writing Test Classes and Methods[136] for an integration on how to write tests in Swift.

Once you have a number of tests written, it is time to start looking at cloud/SaaS based build solutions. Travis[137] is one of my favorites, but also check out BuddyBuild[138], AWS Device Farm[139], BrowserStack[140] or SauceLabs[141].

Experiment with Machine Learning

Apple has released *Core ML 2* which is described in Apple's site[142]) as an *'machine learning framework used across Apple products, including Siri, Camera, and QuickType. Core ML 2 delivers blazingly fast performance with easy integration of machine learning models, enabling you to build apps with intelligent features using just a few lines of code'.*

This means that you can easily add features like *Vision* or *Natural Language* to your application. If you do this, make sure to write

---

[136]https://developer.apple.com/library/archive/documentation/DeveloperTools/Conceptual/testing_with_xcode/chapters/04-writing_tests.html

[137]https://docs.travis-ci.com/user/languages/objective-c/

[138]https://www.buddybuild.com/

[139]https://aws.amazon.com/device-farm/

[140]https://www.browserstack.com/ios-testing

[141]https://saucelabs.com/resources/articles/ios-app-testing

[142]https://developer.apple.com/machine-learning/

blog posts about your experiments, since I'm sure any potential employer would be very interested in reading them.

Publish to AppStore

If you want to take this up a level, you should try to get your application published in the AppStore. This will have some costs, but they will be worth it for the learnings that you will get.

This would also be highly impressive for any potential employer, since it will show that you were able to meet Apple's quality bar.

Dot Language

As a new developer joining the market, one of the real-world patterns that will surprise you the most, is the lack of up-to-date documentation and diagrams about how the applications, services and even code behave (and even when documentation does exists, they are usually out-of-date and not used on day-to-day decisions and coding).

When you take a step back and think about this, you should realise that it is insane. What we do when developing software is to create large interconnected and complex structures without accurate maps, without a solid understanding of what already exists and what we are supposed to be building.

This doesn't happen because developers, architects or managers don't understand or value good up-to-date documentation. In fact they are usually the first ones to complain about these gaps. The problem is that most patterns and technologies used to create these diagrams are highly inefficient, time-consuming, complex and isolated.

DOT[143] is a text based representation of graphs which is a key part of the solution.

---

[143]https://en.wikipedia.org/wiki/DOT_(graph_description_language)

With DOT you describe the graph/diagram in text which is then transformed (by tools like Graphwiz[144] or vis.js[145]) into a diagram.

Here is an example of DOT Language:

```
1  digraph G {
2      size="2";
3      a [label="Foo"];
4      b [shape=box];
5      a -> b -> c [color=blue]
6      b -> d [style=dotted];
7  }
```

Which looks like this when rendered (try this online at GraphvizOnline[146]

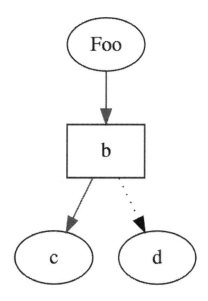

---

[144]http://www.graphviz.org/

[145]http://visjs.org/network_examples.html

[146]https://dreampuf.github.io/GraphvizOnline/

What I'm talking about is 'Diagrams as code', which is a major paradigm shift that very few developers and professionals have been able to make.

As you will see below, text-based representation of reality using diagrams is an area that still needs a lot of innovation and usage. I strongly recommend you to get your head around how to use DOT language for diagraming, since that will give you a strong competitive advantage.

Why we need diagrams

One of the key challenges that exist when working in a team with multiple stake-holders and areas of expertise, is the alignment of what are the objectives and what will be delivered. Don't underestimate how hard this is. Without a graphical representation of the plan and reality, it is very hard to have that alignment. Actually what we really need are Maps[147], but starting with diagrams is a good start.

Diagrams provide an lingua franca[148] to communicate between team members, where they makes it much easier to synchronize expectations, making sure that every stake holder understands the diagram's reality and action plans.

Version control graphs using Git

A key advantage of storing diagram data in a text format, is that you are able to use git to version control them.

The benefits are tremendous, since now you are able to manage your diagrams as you manage your code:

- commit every change

---

[147]https://medium.com/wardleymaps
[148]https://en.wikipedia.org/wiki/Lingua_franca

- branches for new features
- tags to mark releases/sprints
- easily collaborate between multiple team members
- diff between versions (and actually see and understand what changed between versions)

Diff graphs and animate evolution

Your brain is really good at understanding patterns, but due to the highly efficient and hyperlinked way our brains work, what we think we remember from a diagram reviewed a couple days (or weeks) ago, is not usually a good representation of what we actually saw (or think we saw). This becomes a major problem when reviewing diagrams for a 2nd, 3rd or nth time, since unless we are presented with *'what changed since the last review'*, our brains will really struggle to figure it out.

One of the nice side effects of storing diagram data in a text based format, is that diffing versions becomes possible (i.e. it is possible to create text and graphical representations of those changes).

Diffing Diagrams (and making it as easy and smooth process), is is another area that we need quite a bit of innovation and a good area for you to become a player.

Why Visio doesn't scale

But why not use Visio[149], or one of its online/offline variations (like draw.io[150] or Lucidchart[151])?

Visio diagrams are the current industry standard for creating detailed technical and workflow diagrams. The reality is that Visio diagrams can look really good (specially if its creator has good design sense and good taste).

---

[149]https://en.wikipedia.org/wiki/Microsoft_Visio
[150]https://www.draw.io/
[151]https://www.lucidchart.com

The irony is that Visio's main features are actually its main drawbacks. Due to the fact that Visio allows the creation of very detailed diagrams means that it is:

- **very time consuming** - it is normal to take hours (if not days) to create detailed diagrams
- **created from somebody's interpretation of reality** - the author of the Visio diagram will have a massive impact on the design, taxonomies, conventions and depth of detail, which means that it's personal bias and agenda will be reflected in the diagram
- **a work of art** - yes some diagrams look really beautiful, but the point of a diagram is to help with data communication, understanding and collaboration. The point should be to empower decisions, not to look good
- **not created from dynamic data** - all elements in the Visio diagram are manually added, which means that once the original data/scenario/architecture changes, the diagram will be out-of-data
- **layout is pixel based** - which means that moving anything can become really hard because the actually location of a particular element is 'hard-coded' to a particular location in the page (i.e. its pixel). This is one of the reasons why changes are so hard, since it is easy to hit clashes between elements, when moving/adding new elements
- **locked to a particular design convention** - due to the fact that the design is hard-coded and the creator of the Visio diagram has enormous scope for applying its creative interpretation to the diagram's data, what ever convention the author used, becomes the one that everybody has to use. This becomes a massive issue when it is required to see the diagram's data from different points of view or different levels of abstraction
- **very easy to mix abstraction layers** - another common problem with Visio, is the use of multiple abstractions in

the same diagram (for example mixing network flows, with application flows, with user journey flows). This tends to be an side-effect of not being able to reuse part of the diagram in new diagrams for example focused on a particular use-case or user-journey.

- **stored in binary or xml format (very hard to diff)** - not only these files are hard/impossible to diff, some of the file formats are proprietary (i.e. not open) and sometimes on online services the data is not even available.
- **mixes data and design in same file** - to effectively diff data, it is key to store the data and the design in different files. Not only this will make the version diffing possible, it allows the creation of standard design templates (which will create a consistency of design, making it easier to consume)
- **very hard to update** - once a diagram grows to a particular size, simple changes, can required considerate amounts of time (and big changes even more). This creates situations where the diagram authors become 'alergic' to making changes (since they might not have the time required to make the changes)
- **not an accurate representation of reality** - due to the fact that these diagrams are hard to update, even in the unlikely situation that the diagrams were accurate on day 0 (i.e. when they were completed for the first time), due to the natural rate of change in development and systems, it is inevitable that the diagrams will start to go out of date. Then, unless they are significant efforts put in maintaining those diagrams, they stop being sources of truth (and valuable for teams)
- **not used everyday (by developers, architects or managers)** - usually the reason for all the properties listed above, is the simple fact that the diagram's created are not part of the multiple day-to-day conversations and decisions that occur between the multiple players
- **they are usually not maps** - finally the worse part of 99% of the diagrams out there is that that are not Maps. Although

diagrams tend to be visual, have context (i.e. specific to purpose / perspective) and are mode of components , they miss
the key mapping properties[152] of: anchor, position (relative to
anchor) and consistency of movement.

Not being able to control the layout is a feature

When you start using text based diagraming tools (like DOT) one
of the behaviors that will drive you crazy is the fact that you
can't control the diagram layout (in the same way you do in
Visio). Text based diagrams are dynamically rendered based on a
set of predefined strategies. This means that the exact location of
components will vary with most changes (note that some engines
allow the fixation of components, which allows the creation of
anchors and special areas).

This limitation is actually the **best feature** of text base diagrams!

It is only when you stop caring about the exact layout that you
realise that it doesn't really matter, since as long as you understand
the diagram's context, they are easy to read and consume.

The other positive site effect of this lack of control, is the fact that
changes (big or small) are easy to make, which means that it is easy
to keep the diagrams up-to-date.

Automatic generation of graphs for code

So what is the solution to make diagrams scale so that they are:

- a correct representation of reality
- easy to create and maintain
- able to provide multiple views from the same data
- able to separate code and data
- easy to diff (between versions)

---

[152]http://wardleypedia.org/mediawiki/index.php/Wardley_Mapping

The solution is to auto-generate the diagrams (from source-code, config files, data-analysis, logs, or other data sources). Only then will we have something that can be maintained and correctly represents reality.

But doesn't this mean that we need a way to parse the (for example) config files, understand its structure and find a way to create information from it?

Yes

And what is wrong with being able to do that ?

What is crazy is to make decisions based on shadows of reality (or even worse, what somebody thinks reality is)

Infrastructure as Code

One of the good things of codifying the infrastructure (vs clicking on things or running a bunch of scripts), is that it provides the opportunity to use the config/recipe files to generate diagrams that represent what they create.

A good example is the visualization of the relationships between multiple running Docker containers. In Docker based environments, when this visualization of running containers is not available (in quasi real-time), eventually, it will become really hard to understand what is really going on. This this is reason why system failures caused by cascading set of events, start to become a common occurrence.

Use Threat Models as a way to create diagrams

Threat Models[153] are a technique used by application security professionals to map out the security implications of a particular design. There are multiple schools of though on how to do threat models.

---

[153]https://en.wikipedia.org/wiki/Threat_model

I like the simple one where we create a set of architecture/flow diagrams and map a number of threads to it: Authentication, Authorization, Data Validation, Secrets Management, Resilience and Privacy. To scale the creation of the Threat Models needs to be done by Security Champions (which are usually developers embedded in a particular team)

The trick here is to use Threat Models as a way to create diagrams that not only represent reality, but are kept up-to-date (by the Security Champion)

And why do teams find the time to do Threat Models, when they struggle to get management/business-buy-in for doing documentation?

Because doing documentation feels like a 'low/medium priority' task (when compared with the latest feature requested by the business), which is easy to keep pushing to one of the 'next sprints'. This is a typical technical debt problem, where the real impact of not doing something will only happen in the future (usually when the ones making the current decisions are not there any more)

But NOT doing a Threat Model, means that that team (namely the business and technical owners) have taken an active step to *'Not understand the security implications of the current design or latest set of changes'*. This is a much higher risk and one that if you have a mature risk based workflow, will create a set of vulnerabilities and risks for those technical and management owners to accept (which is exactly what we do at Photobox Group Security).

The crazy idea that in Agile you don't need documentation

...To go fast, you can go alone

...To go far, you need to go in a team

...To go fast and far, you need to go in a team and have real-time understanding/visualization of what is being created/executed

One of the very dangerous ideas that started to happen in Agile teams that were able to deploy fast to production, was the idea that *you don't need to document and diagrams things* (since that will just slow things down).

This is a crazy idea and very short-sighted!

The quality of the test code and ability to create diagrams from what actually exists, are critical factors in creating highly productive, effective and rewarding environments.

People, Process and Technology

The biggest challenge in adopting (for example) DOT Language, are the *People* and *Process* part.

Although there still are some limitations in the *Technology* part (for example DOT diagrams need to have better support for icons, and provide better control of the positioning/anchor of key components), what I find is the hardest part, is for the *People* to do the paradigm shifts mentioned in this chapter.

Once they do, the *Processes* will evolve around the existing tech stack (for reference the tech stack I use is: DOT Language, Git, GitHub, Vis.js and Hugo)

Evolution of Diagrams into Maps

What is very frustrating is that in most development teams, we are still at the *'Why do we need up-to-date diagrams?'* phase.

Where the question that we should be looking at is *'How can we make our diagrams every better and more valuable?'*

And the answer is Maps, which are diagrams with the following properties

- are visual

- have context (i.e. specific to purpose / perspective)
- are mode of components
- have at least one anchor
- have a position (relative to anchor)
- have a consistency of movement

For a great introduction to this kind of maps see Wardley Mapping[154], which was created by Simon Wardley who is writing a book about it[155] at Medium.

Explore Vis.js Javascript engine

If you are looking for a great javascript-based DOT language visualization engine, then *vis.js network*[156] is the one I recommend you spend a lot of time learning and customizing (see my neovis fork[157] for an example of what those customization can look like)

Mermaid and WebSequenceDiagrams.com

Another good example of diagram as code is the open source Mermaid[158] tool, which is designed to help with chart generation.

Here is what a Sequence Diagram code looks like in Mermaid

---

[154]http://wardleypedia.org/mediawiki/index.php/Wardley_Mapping
[155]https://medium.com/wardleymaps
[156]http://visjs.org/docs/network/
[157]https://github.com/pbx-gs/neovis.js
[158]https://mermaidjs.github.io/

```
1  sequenceDiagram
2      participant Alice
3      participant Bob
4      Alice->John: Hello John, how are you?
5      loop Healthcheck
6          John->John: Fight against hypochondria
7      end
8      Note right of John: Rational thoughts <br/>prev\
9  ail...
10      John-->Alice: Great!
11      John->Bob: How about you?
12      Bob-->John: Jolly good!
```

Which looks like this when rendered:

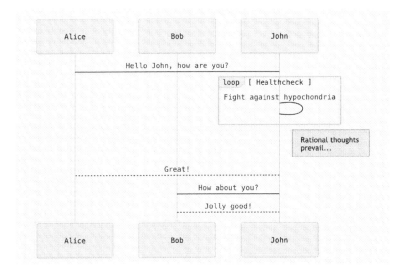

An alternative is the proprietary https://www.websequencediagrams.com service, which more feature rich that mermaid and has a nicer design (the free version is already very usable and practical):

```
1   title Authentication Sequence
2
3   Alice->Bob: Authentication Request
4   note right of Bob: Bob thinks about it
5   Bob->Alice: Authentication Response
```

Will look like this

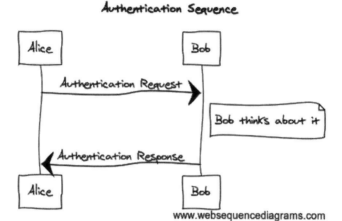

The Diagram in R[159] integration page contains a great video of DOT in action:

---

[159]http://rich-iannone.github.io/DiagrammeR/index.html

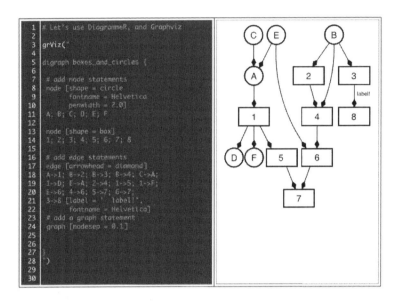

Btw, if you have not learned how to code in R^{160}, you definitely should, since it is a great way to manipulate and visualise data).

Try it! (learn DOT and Mermaid with real-time preview)

A good tech stack to learn DOT Language (and mermaid) is the Atom editor[161] with the Markdown Preview Enhanced[162] package installed.

This is create an REPL[163] environment where you have an highly effective and productive split screen (on the left you have the markdown page, and on the right the rendered page/diagram). Once you make a code change, you will see the rendered diagram in less than a second. This workflow makes it really easy to learn and to create diagrams in real-time.

---

[160]https://en.wikipedia.org/wiki/R_(programming_language)

[161]https://atom.io/

[162]https://atom.io/packages/markdown-preview-enhanced

[163]https://en.wikipedia.org/wiki/Read%E2%80%93eval%E2%80%93print_loop

I have done Threat Modeling sessions in the past, where we have the UI described above projected on a wall, which allow us to create the diagrams in real-time, based on the information provided by the meeting attendees.

Wallaby and NCrunch

WallabyJS[164] is a an *Integrated Continuous Testing Tool for JavaScript* that represents the best TDD (Test Driven Development) environment that I've seen, because it allows the creation of a highly productive and efficient development workflow. NCrunch[165] is very similar for .NET and all the concepts below also apply to it (my experience is that wallaby is a bit faster). Unfortunately there isn't an equivalent for the other languages (some IDEs do have the ability to automatically execute tests, but they only have subset of the features I describe below and the development experience is not the same)

WallabyJS is an plugin/add-on for the most popular IDEs (Web-Storm, IntelliJ IDEA, PhpStorm, Rider, RubyMine, PyCharm, Visual Studio , Atom Text Editor, Sublime Text) that enables the execution of Unit Tests immediately. The loop from detection to 'test execution completion', usually takes less than 1 sec, which give it a feel of real-time test execution.

The proof of a good piece of technology is when it dramatically improves the productivity of its users by changing how they behave and operate (while making them awesome). WallabyJS and NCrunch are such technologies, and it is key that you as a developer understand why, and learn how to use it (or its patterns).

---

[164]https://wallabyjs.com/
[165]https://www.ncrunch.net/

All developers test their code

One key concept that I always try to make to developers, is that they are already testing their code changes. Then tend to do these tests in a highly inefficient way, but they are still testing their code and their changes.

For example when developers make a change in a particular web page or back-end service, they will fire up a browser or PostMan and click a number of times until their reach the location where the change they made can be seen in action.

The problem is that in most cases the ways they test their changes:

- Are highly inefficient
- Can take many seconds or event minutes to test one change
- Are hard to repeat and Ephemeral[166]
- Are limited in their scope (i.e. not testing most/all real-world moving parts affected by the changes)
- Tend to focus on a very narrow set of use-cases
- Lose the history of the multiple tests scenario tested
- Make the developer switch context in their mind
- Do not show the code coverage (in the IDE) of the changes made (seconds after the test complete)

The reality is that developing using workflows that don't have the capabilities enabled by WallabyJS is highly expensive, inefficient, unproductive, slow, and frustrating for everybody involved (namely the developers who pay the price of that inefficiency every time they code, and the users who don't get a fast turn around for the features they want)

---

[166]https://en.wiktionary.org/wiki/ephemeral

Key WallabyJS features

As with everything, the key is in the People, Process and Technology ecosystem.

WallabyJS is a *Technology* that enables a massive paradigm shift in the *People* involved, that leads to massive changes in the *Process* of testing and developing applications.

Here are the key features that WallabyJS has (that I wished every IDE had by default):

- **Automatic execution of tests** - as soon as you make a change to the code (or save it), the tests runs automatically (WallabyJS is so fast, that some tests actually execute in between your key stokes)
- **Execution of only affected tests** - part of making the automatic execution of tests scale is the ability to only execute the tests that were changed. The ability to detect this also means that there is no need to keep configuring the test runner
- **Execution of only tests affected by code changes** - this feature answers the question *"what is the impact of the code change I just made"*. Using code coverage, it is possible to know the tests that are currently able to hit the lines that where changed (and then only execute those). This is such a simple concept, but makes a massive difference, since the alternative is to run all tests or to try to manually find the tests that can be executed.
- **Code coverage in the IDE after execution** - Another feature highly underestimated is the power of seeing in the IDE the status of the test's execution. Not only this clearly shows the areas of the code that are currently not being reached, the way WallabyJS (and NCrunch) do it is very cleaver, since they show the paths of pass and fail (i.e. you see in green the lines that were executed by passing tests, and in red the lines affected by failed tests). This allows for really

powerful workflows, including a massive reduction of the need to 'debug' code using a 'debugger'. In many projects that I was involved in, after a while, we realized that me and development team stopped using the debugger when coding! Wallaby or NCrunch gave us enough visibility to understand where the bug was (this allowed us to not have to deal with all the inefficient of having to maintain a salad of breakpoints and hundreds of 'Step Into' or 'Step Over' clicks)

- **Feedback of values in IDE** - A nice little feature of WallabyJS is that it has a number of ways to get feedback from the tests being executed. This goes from simple `console.log` outputs to expressions and even variable transformations, that are showed directly in the IDE and in context.

- **Crazy fast execution** - Is easy to underestimate the speed of execution of WallabyJS, and fail to realise that it is one of the core reasons that makes WallabyJS so effective and empowering. In fact I thought that NCrunch was fast, but after using WallabyJS for a while, NCrunch felt really slow, and using normal test runners just kills my brain. We have quite a lot of data on how page speed affects users experience (see *Why Performance Maters*[167]) and it is the same for test execution and the developer's brain. When tests execute automatically and in less than a second, there is a flow and effectiveness that occurs, which dramatically improves productivity and focus.

Aim for 100% code coverage

My view of code coverage is that if you make a change in the code and a test didn't break, you are making random changes (where you don't really understand the side effects of your changes).

Even when you are doing refactoring, you should break a number of tests until you arrive back a test passing state.

---

[167]https://developers.google.com/web/fundamentals/performance/why-performance-matters/

This means that you need to aim for 100% code coverage, since that means that all of your code is covered by tests. I know that this high-code-coverage percentage can be gamed, and there are many horror stories on companies that abused this metric (which always are indicators of bigger problems within the development culture and management).

If fact, what you want is much more than code coverage. What you want is to make sure that the tests that are executed, correctly represent your understanding of what the code changed is doing.

This means that the question is not *"When I made this change, did a test break?"* but it should be instead *"When I made this change, did the tests that failed represent my understanding of the change I made"*.

The bottom line is that if you make changes to parts of your code that are not reflected in tests, then how do you know that your changes/fixes worked as expected?

The only way to achieve this level of code coverage is to expose the developer to real-time code-coverage in the IDE (i.e. the developer is able to see exactly what lines and code have coverage, and even more interesting, which ones have been affected by the code changes)

Wallaby represents the real TDD

One of the unfortunate side-effects of the horror stories of high code coverage exercises (namely the ones that created massive white-elephants that were completely unusable and very expensive to maintain), is the allergic reaction that TDD (Test Driven Development) can sometimes have today.

What ended up happening is that everybody agrees that TDD is very important, that TDD is should be used by all developers, that TDD is an important factor in the hiring and candidate selection process, but when we look at where TDD is actually used, we tend to see that it happens on low level 'pure' Unit Tests, and code coverages of 80%+ are seen as a success.

Part of the problem is how TDD is perceived to work. The bad (in my point of view) workflow that tends to be described as TDD is:

1. Start with a passing state
2. Write a failed test with the smallest possible feature
3. make a code change that makes that test pass
4. back to 1 (until the function does what it is supposed to do)

The problem is that this is only useful and relevant in a couple of the TDD scenarios.

The way I do TDD is

1. Start with a passing state
2. Make a change (in production code or in an test)
3. Fix the code or tests (so that we are back into the passing state)
4. Back to 1 (until the feature does what it is supposed to do)

Although the 1st and last steps are the same, the middle bit is very important.

I like to view it as *I'm pair programming with myself*, where I loop back and forward from code and tests.

What matters is that the code changes are made in the location that matters the most at that moment in time. Also important is that I use this workflow for everything, from tests that affect a stand alone function (traditional called an *Unit Tests*), to tests that require quite a bit of code and state to be executed in order to really test the changes (traditionally called *Integration Tests*).

For me a *Test* is the confirmation that a particular behavior exists in a particular scenario (which can be a function, an web service, an website, an CI pipeline, an Docker container, an Cloud setup, etc..).

Basically a Test is an answer to an Question. The more questions you have the better you will be. The objective is to achieve the widest possible range of scenarios and code coverage. In fact a really good measure would be to track how much code a test actually touched (the higher value, the better)

A good sign that TDD has lost is mojo, is the fact that code coverage effectiveness is not usually mapped to an team's deliverables or OKRs (Objectives and Key Results). Development teams will respond to the reward's systems set in place. If we don't reward the creation of highly effective test environments with high degrees of code coverage, then we shouldn't be surprised when that doesn't happen.

I keep trying to find a better name for the workflow that WallabyJs enables, but TDD still feels like the correct term, since when I code using WallabyJS I am really doing Test Driven Development.

FDD (Feedback Driven Development) is a close alternately, but TDD is still the one I like the most.

Test code is as important as production code

I will argue that focusing on the quality of your test code is as important as focusing on the quality of the code that you actually run in production.

Why? because the more effective and productive your test code and test environment is, the better your production code will be. But the opposite is not true (i.e. the better your production code is, doesn't mean that the better your test code will be).

If your team doesn't not have the same amount of care and craftsmanship with test code as they have with production code (including testing the test pipeline), then you will never achieve the speeds and quality of development that are desired.

Part of the problem seems to be the horror stories caused by big and cumbersome test environments that actually slowed teams down (where a couple minutes 'code changes' required hours of 'test changes'). This is a symptom of badly engineered test environments and lack of time spending on improving the test infrastructure and effectiveness.

As a developer, your test environment (and executing workflow) is one of the most important capabilities that you need to work on (and improve). Just like successful athletes put a massive amount of energy and focus in their supporting equipment, you as a developer need to make sure that the code that helps you to write good production code, is as effective and robust as possible (see *How 1% Performance Improvements Led to Olympic Gold*[168])

You have to try it to believe it

As with everything, the best way to learn is to experience it, so download one of the Open Source editors (like Atom[169] or VS Code[170]), install the Evaluation version of WallabyJS and give it a good test drive.

Try it in some of the apps that you are coding, or write something new. What is important is that you experience the power of *'real-time test execution and code coverage'*.

Another good use of WallabyJS is to understand how an API works. One of the patterns I follow when learning how to use a new API, is to write tests that invoke its capabilities. Not only this allows me to gain a much better understanding of how that API works, the tests I leave behind, represent my understanding of that API at that moment in time, and more importantly, how I expected that API to behave. This is very important in helping to detect future bugs

---

[168]https://hbr.org/2015/10/how-1-performance-improvements-led-to-olympic-gold
[169]https://atom.io/
[170]https://code.visualstudio.com/

caused by modifications in that API's behavior (caused by upgrades or security fixes)

When learning how to use WallabyJS you are exploring the concept Bret Victor mentions in his Inventing on principle[171] presentation which is the 'The need for inventors to be close to what they create and have quick feedback'

Why isn't wallabyJS more widely used

For me, once I saw and experienced NCrunch and then WallabyJS, I knew that I would never be able to code in .Net or Javascript without having access to those capabilities.

But the question that really puzzles me, is why its adoption is still quite low?

Why aren't more developers using it and why aren't they demanding the IDE's developers to add those features? This is one of the reasons why IDE support for these workflows is so low, there isn't enough market pressure.

One reason could be a general lack of investment in tools for developers. In some companies that is seen as a cost, instead of an investment. I've seen companies that are happy to hire a new developer for £60k, but don't seem to have the budget to spend the same amount in tools for existing developers (where that £60k would have a much bigger impact)

But even in companies what are ok with investing on developer's tools (and wallaby isn't that expensive, since it costs $100 per named developer or $240 for a company license), I still don't see developers asking for those licenses. Why is that?

My only logical explanation is the natural resistance to change, an lack of understanding of the power of these kind of testing

---

[171]https://vimeo.com/36579366

environments/workflows, and a lack of time to make WallabyJS work in the current application.

Usually the argument is that *'It sounds good but we are too busy to improve the test environment'*, which is a self fulfilling tragedy, since until the test environment is improved, everybody is always going to be busy and reactive.

As a new developer, this blind spot is a massive opportunity for you. If you are able to make these paradigm changes, and behave in a real TDD way, you just gained a massive competitive advantage in the market place.

We need an Wallaby for the Cloud

One of the side effects of current lack of efforts in making new technologies easy to test (I mean in an WallabyJS-like workflow, since we have moved a long way from the old completely un-testable APIs, like the early versions of .NET or Java web stacks), is that we are not adding these *'real-time test and code-coverage'* capabilities to the new tech stacks.

For example who is writing tests for their *'Infrastructure as Code'* scripts?

- How do we know that code used to setup an cloud environment is actually working as expected?
- How do we know that the Auto-Scaling set-up is actually working as expected?
- How do we know that an DNS change is not causing massive side effects in an unrelated part of the application?
- How do we know that the upgrade, crash or misbehavior of Service X, actually causes an unexpected massive disruption in Service Y? (which btw is one of the questions that Chaos Engineering tries to answer)

- Who is writing tests for Serverless functions, for example Lambdas? I don't mean tests that run locally, I mean tests that actually run on the Serverless environment?

What is really nice about making the paradigm shifts mentioned in the chapter, is that your brain will refuse to program in any other way. So when recently I had to write some Lambda functions in Python, after realising that the maturity of the Lambda TDD environment was really low, I spend a bit of time creating an environment where using the AWS boto3's API (which wraps most AWS capabilities in easy to use Python functions) I was able to create an environment in PyCharm[172] where I could execute lambdas (written locally) in AWS in less than 1 sec.

Since PyCharm has a feature to auto execute the last test after a couple seconds of a code change, I was able to create an workflow where 2 seconds after making a code change, the affected Lambda was executed in AWS (with execution times under 1 second). Ok it is not as effective as WallabyJS and I don't get code coverage, but it is much better than anything else I saw (from tools that created local simulated AWS Lambda environments in Docker, to tools like Serverless that used CloudFormation to deploy the Lambdas and took almost 1 minute to run)

The problem of switching context

Part of the reason WallabyJS-Driven-Development makes such a difference, is because it prevents your brain from doing Context Switching.

Our brains are not very good at switching context, which is why even a couple seconds interruption can be so damaging.

When we program, what we are doing is creating in our brains a whole set of model models about the problem/issue we are addressing. This is why sometimes we can be super productive, and other

---

[172]https://www.jetbrains.com/pycharm/

times, we just can't make it work. This is key in programing since the impact of bad/inefficient code can be enormous. Sometimes it's much better not to code, than to write code that will cause so many side-effects at later stage, that those code changes actually had a negative value (i.e. like when somebody is trying to help, but they are actually 'anti-help').

This is also why it is very important to have un-interrupted periods of time for coding (ideally blocks of 2 or 4 hours), since it takes a while to build these mental models and gain speed.

When we code in an non WallabyJS-Driven-Development environnement, what happens is that we are forced to switch context every time we want to test an code change. Even if that is only a couple seconds of mouse clicks or keyboard strokes, the compound effect of that interruption is enormous. This is way worse when the time that it takes to start the test is more than 10 seconds or even minutes (the impact of productivity is enormous)

With an WallabyJS-Driven-Development environment, what happens is that you get into a groove (or flow), where you are able to focus 100% on the code that you are writing. You will also start to use the visual feedback that you get from WallabyJS as part of your development. You need to experience this to understand but, when you get this right, this is what being the 'coding zone' really feels like, and the productivity that you achieve is really something incredible.

One question I'm asked quite a lot is *How can I code and learn so fast*. The answer is in how I code and the time I spend in creating productive environments that allow me to code and learn in the 'Zone'.

As a developer if you can behave like this, you will have a massive competitive advantage in the marketplace, specially when applying for new jobs. It is very common these days to ask job applicants to write some tests during an job interview. Guess who will stand out in those interviews and get the job?

One to watch: LightTable

As a final idea, if I were you, I would spend some time with the experimental LightTable[173] Open Source IDE (ideally even becoming a contributor)

I need to give this tool a better test drive, but it looks really promising. since it has implemented a number of the features presented in Bret Victor's *Inventing on principle*[174] video, namely the real time feedback of code changes and showing the values in the IDE.

One area I would like to see more examples/use-cases is how LightTable can be to applied to testing, which is a good area for you to focus your research on :)

---

[173]http://lighttable.com/
[174]https://vimeo.com/36579366

Technologies

Another important technologies to know.

Books

I love books, the 'real world' physical ones, the BookBook[175](s). Not the digital alternatives who are a shadow of a book and are not good technologies to consume knowledge.

I love books, and for a while I too had the a guilty feeling of 'holding on to legacy technology', as the world moved into consuming more and more digital content (including digital books).

For reference I buy hundreds of books per year and spend far too much money than I should on books. Have I read them all, no of course not! Have I found amazing books to read every year that improved my skills and knowledge, absolutely yes!!! The reason I buy so many books (multiple per topic) is because until I start reading them, I don't know which one is perfect (at that moment in time)

After looking closely at why I liked books so much, I had the epiphany[176] that *"Books are actually the best technology to consume and process information"*.

There is also a growing body of research that shows that the use of digital technologies are also affecting kid's learning capabilities (see "students find it easier to read and learn from printed materials[177]")

---

[175]https://medium.com/r/?url=https%3A%2F%2Fwww.youtube.com%2Fwatch%3Fv%3DMOXQo7nURs0

[176]http://blog.diniscruz.com/2013/09/physical-books-are-best-technology-for.html

[177]https://twitter.com/nicolekearney/status/963946721662267392

Basically, if you don't use books or printed materials to read and review the information you are consuming (and creating), you are missing a massive trick.

The digital world is really good at promoting group think[178] and to present the previous technologies as 'legacy' and old-fashioned.

My experience is that books (and printed materials) are much better technologies for the consumption of information. One area where the advantages of the digital books can be significant are novels and fictional stories (namely the convenience of access and the weight difference), in this case the books are just a transient medium that is being used to tell a story, just like in a movie (in most cases, what the reader is getting are emotional connections with the characters/story, and not really learning from the text)

The reality is if you want to learn, you are better of using a book or printed materials.

The same happens with reviewing materials. It not coincidence that we all have experiences of writing content in a digital medium (i.e. the computer) and while reading it on a screen it kinda looks ok. Then once we print it, and enjoy the unidirectional, offline and 100% focused activity experience that is 'reading a piece of paper', we find tons of errors and 'WTF was I thinking when I wrote that!' moments. In fact making notes on printed versions of digital content, is exactly how I am writing and reviewing this book's content.

Yes, the fact that books are offline is one of the book's main competitive advantages!

The book's 'features' of not being interrupted by a constant stream of apps/websites notifications and not having a browser at hand, does wonders for your ability to focus and to consume information.

Another powerful feature of books (in addition of rendering con-tentin HD with real-time refresh rate), is that they allow your brain

---

[178]https://en.wikipedia.org/wiki/Groupthink

to consume information in a 3D format and with more senses. For example, notice how when you flick back pages looking for a particular passage or diagram, your eyes will be looking at a particular section of the page. This means that your brain not only is capturing the content that it is reading, it is also capturing (and storing) the location of that content, and how it relates to the rest of the page. One of the reasons that lead me to the epiphany of the value of books was how I noticed that it was bothering me the fact that the kindle reorders paragraphs and pages when you flick back (and how it was affecting my ability to find content I've already read)

Environmental impact of books

My understanding (and please correct me if I'm wrong) is that most books these are are printed from either recycled paper or from sustainable forests (i.e. forests where they plant at least as many new trees as they cut).

This mean that these days, the impact of books on the environment is minimal.

Pen and Paper

Another powerful technology that seems to be going out of fashion is the pen and paper (pencil is also a great option).

As covered in the 'Book' chapter, analogue techniques like the pen and paper are actually better technologies for creating and capturing ideas.

The fact that a piece of paper (or notebook) is not 'online' and one cannot easily change its contents, are actually some of its best features.

What is really important is to capture the ideas and thoughts that you have. There are also studies that shows that just the fact that you write something, will make it easier for you to remember and to process that information.

I have so many examples of situations when I started writing just some ideas, and after a couple pages, the real interesting ideas come out (due to the hyperlinked nature of how ideas are generated in the brain). What is important is the realisation that those 2nd or 3rd generation of ideas would had not been captured without the first batch of ideas and notes. I've also found that my brain retains the location of where I made some notes, and I'm able to go back to those notebooks and remember what where those ideas (even after a couple years).

These days, to keep track of what I have reviewed and processed, I have the workflow/habit or crossing-over the ideas or texts that I moved to a digital format or delegated.

The reality is that you will forget the ideas you are having today!

The only way to make sure that your future self has access to those ideas, is to capture them now!

It is great when you review your older notebooks (could be from last week or year) and not only remember an idea you had since forgotten, but you are able to expand that idea and take it to the next level.

My favourite are the Moleskin books[179] plain A5 notebooks, since they represent a nice balance of white space and portability (I use them everyday)

A nice side effect of having mobile phones with cameras, is that it's easy to share a picture of one of the notebook's pages.

---

[179]https://www.amazon.co.uk/Moleskine-Sapphire-Large-Plain-Notebook/dp/B015NG45Q0/

Assembly and Bytecode

Assembly code is a representation of what the machine code that the CPUs actually execute. It is the lowest level of abstraction that you can program.

The moment I fell in love with programming was when (as a teenager) I executed the POKE assembly command in my ZX Spectrum, which changed a pixel on my TV screen. That was such a magical moment because I had direct control over what was happening inside the computer and screen.

PEEK and POKE[180] were BASIC[181] commands that allow direct memory access and manipulation (PEEK reads and POKE writes). What I was doing was to write directly to the memory location that was used to control the screen (i.e. each byte in that memory address represented a small section of the screen).

A while later I started learning how to go deeper and explored writing assembly code. In those 'pre internet' days there was very little information around and with only one book available, I actually remember manually translating assembly code into binary by hand (I didn't started with an assembler compiler). Eventually I got an assembler and did many experiments in the ZX Spectrum, the Amiga 500[182] and the x86 PCs (which when compared with the Amiga's Motorola 68000 microprocessor had a much more complex memory layout).

In fact my first 'security hacks' were based around memory and disk manipulations written in assembly. They were designed to manipulate and change the behavior of the games I was playing (I think there was some cool way to get more money in SimCity)

Looking back, what I can see is that when I was writing assembly language, what I was doing was learning (in a very efficient way)

---

[180]https://en.wikipedia.org/wiki/PEEK_and_POKE
[181]https://en.wikipedia.org/wiki/BASIC
[182]https://en.wikipedia.org/wiki/Amiga_500

about: computer architecture, memory layout, systems design, programming and much more. For example learning about hardware interrupts, TSR (Terminate and Stay Resident), and Kernel vs Userland memory, did wonders for my understanding of computer science.

These days you are more likely to code in Python, Java or .Net than assembly. But if you look under the hood, these languages are compiled into bytecode[183] which is a normalized version of assembly.

For example here is what `print("Hello, World!")` looks like in python's bytecode[184]

```
1   0 LOAD_NAME        0 (print)
2   2 LOAD_CONST       0 ('Hello, World!')
3   4 CALL_FUNCTION    1
```

Python (as with .Net and Java) is a stack-based virtual machine[185] which is provides a translation layer between the language and the CPU specific machine code

Decompiling code

Bytecode is the reason why .Net and Java can be easily decompiled from an .dll or .class file.

In .Net this can be quite spectacular since tools like ILSpy[186] allow the easy decompilation of non-obfuscated .Net assembly (including the ones from the Microsoft .Net Framework).

For viewing C++ and other compiled code, two great tools on windows are ollydbg[187] and Ida Pro[188]

---

[183]https://en.wikipedia.org/wiki/Bytecode
[184]https://opensource.com/article/18/4/introduction-python-bytecode
[185]https://en.wikipedia.org/wiki/Stack_machine
[186]https://github.com/icsharpcode/ILSpy
[187]http://www.ollydbg.de
[188]https://www.hex-rays.com/products/ida/

Brain

How well do you know your brain? Do you know how it works? What areas it is really strong at, what areas it is weak and how to maximise its capabilities?

The human brain is one of the world's great wonders and we live in a age where we now know a tremendous amount of details on how it works.

You need understand how your brain work, so that you understand it's blind spots and why we behave in the way we do.

How do you think? How do you remember? How do you see? How rational are your decisions? Who is actually making the decisions in your head?

If you have not looked at this topic before, you will be very surprised with the answers to these questions.

As a developer your brain is your tool. What makes you special and different from other developers is your ability to create mental models, process information, codify your intentions and execute your ideas.

This is where you need to apply your logical and computing side of the brain and reverse engineer how your own brain works.

I've always found the brain fascinating and the more I learned about it, the better I become at understanding how I and others think.

A good place to start is the Freakonomics: A Rogue Economist Explores the Hidden Side of Everything[189] book, which uses economic techniques to answer a number of very interesting questions.

The Predictably Irrational: The Hidden Forces That Shape Our

---

[189]https://www.amazon.co.uk/Freakonomics-Economist-Explores-Hidden-Everything/dp/0141019018

Decisions[190] takes that to another level, where it shows example after example how we are not rational at all in a number of decisions we make everyday

The best one I've read is Incognito - The Secret lives of the brain[191] which not only explains really well how the brain works, it really challenges our understanding of how the brain works.

How I think

When self analysing how I think (from an engineering point of view), I found that I have two types of thinking techniques.

- A slow(ish) type of thinking - where I'm basically talking to myself in my head. This is also how I tend to read (I heard the text I'm reading in my head)
- A fast type of thinking - where I 'somehow' am making a large number of analysis and decisions, and 'know' what I'm thinking without really needing to articulate in my head all the explanations of what I'm doing. This is the kind of thinking that one tends to get when in 'the Zone' (which is that magical place where ideas 'just flow' and we are hyper productive)

The more time you can spend on the 2nd type the more productive you will be.

I've also found that although my brain is able to hold a large amount of hyperlinked information (creating a graph of linked data that I'm working on), it is not good at all at multi-tasking (i.e. working on multiple domain problems at the same time or performing a manual activity).

This is why is so important to be able to spend concentrated time on a particular topic, since it takes a while to upload all relevant data to the parts of the brain focused on the task at hand.

---

[190]https://www.amazon.co.uk/Predictably-Irrational-Hidden-Forces-Decisions/dp/0007256531

[191]https://www.amazon.co.uk/Incognito-Secret-Lives-Brain-Canons/dp/1782112464

Switching context and interruptions

A reason why even a 1 second interruption can be massively disruptive (for example a text message, or slack/snapchat/instragram/facebook/twitter notification) is because it breaks the mojo of your brain and destroys a number of those hyperlinked graphs you had created in your head.

It is even worse when the interruption actually requires some extra activity (for example a question from somebody at the office).

One area that these interruptions happen a lot in the normal developer's coding workflow is Testing. The simple fact of having to manually run a test (either via the command line, or by clinking on a web browser), will break your mental models and make you 'switch context'

I can't explain (you need to experience it yourself) how productive is it to code in an environment where the context switching is minimal (which is what happens when coding using tools like wallbyjs[192] or NCrunch[193])

IDE

We need to talk about your IDE! (Integrated development environment)

How much time have you spent: choosing it, customizing it, making it suit your development workflow, making it automate actions that you do as a developer, making it automatically execute tests

Your IDE is one of the most important tools in your arsenal and the more time you spend looking after it, the better a programmer you will be:

The IDE is like a car in a race that you are the driver. You really need to spend time caring about it, since your performance as a

---

[192]wallabyjs.com
[193]http://www.ncrunch.net/

developer will be affected by how effective your IDE is for the task at hand

Note that this doesn't mean that the most feature rich IDE will be better. You need to pick the best tool for the job: - for example Visual Studio has tons of features but that made it quite slow (and Windows specific), which is why other editors (like Atom) started to gain traction. Microsoft then released VS Code which is much more lightweight and effective. - Sometimes Notepad or Vim are the best IDES - I quite like the JetBrains suite of tools (WebStorm for Node , PyCharm for Python and IntelliJ for Java) - Eclipse can also be a great editor (specially if you customize it) - Cloud IDEs (like Cloud9) can be amazing in some cases (in one project I had a special docker instance that added Cloud9 to a node application)

One of the key requirements for me in the IDE is the ability to:

- run tests quickly (once you stopped typing)
- run tests affected by the latest code changes
- show code coverage in the IDE

At the moment the only place where I have seen those features happening is in NCrunch (for .NET) and WallabyJS (for node/-javascript). The auto test execution capability that some IDEs have, are a decent compromise, but not as effective (and productive as those two tools)

The key point is that you need to take the time and care to chose your IDE, since it has the power to dramatically increase your productivity

Machine Learning and AI

One of the most important areas that you need to gain a strong understanding in the next 5 years is Machine Learning and Artificial Intelligence (AI).

This is not about an Skynet[194] kinda scenario where an super-intelligence singularity[195] is going to take over the world and destroy humanity.

This is about the next major revolution in technology and whether you are going to be a player or a pawn in what is happening next.

I highly recommend that you read Kevin Kelly's The Inevitable: Understanding the 12 Technological Forces That Will Shape Our Future[196] book where he provides a really clean mapping of what (most likely) will happen next.

One area that Kevin talks in detail and you can already see it happening around us is the introduction of AI capabilities in all sort of devices and business activities.

This is where you need to take a proactive approach and start learning about how all this works and how to program it.

The great news is that in the last couple years the major cloud providers have been investing really hard on these technologies and are now providing environments where you can easily play around and learn how machine learning and AI works

See for example all the different tools and technolgies that AWS is already offering in the machine learning[197] space (Microsoft is also providing some really cool capabilities on Azure[198])

As a developer, you will be soon be asked to write code that integrates with Machine Learning technology to process large amounts of data or to integrate an app with AI services like voice, image recognition or domain-specific analysis (for example in medicine)

Where are we going

For a nice view of what could be happening next see:

---

[194]https://en.wikipedia.org/wiki/Skynet_(Terminator)

[195]https://en.wikipedia.org/wiki/Technological_singularity

[196]https://www.amazon.co.uk/Inevitable-Understanding-Technological-Forces-Future/dp/0525428089

[197]https://aws.amazon.com/machine-learning/

[198]https://azure.microsoft.com/en-gb/overview/machine-learning/

- Life 3.0: Being Human in the Age of Artificial Intelligence[199]
- Homo Deus: A Brief History of Tomorrow[200]
- What Technology Wants[201]

AST (Abstract Syntax Tree)

AST[202] (Abstract Syntax Tree) is a graph representation of source code primarily used by compilers to read code and generate the target binaries.

For example, the AST of this code sample: `while b ≠ 0 if a > b a := a - b else b := b - a return a` Will look like this:

---

[199]https://www.amazon.co.uk/Life-3-0-Being-Artificial-Intelligence/dp/024123719X/

[200]https://www.amazon.co.uk/Homo-Deus-Brief-History-Tomorrow/dp/1910701874

[201]https://www.amazon.co.uk/What-Technology-Wants-Kevin-Kelly/dp/0143120174

[202]https://en.wikipedia.org/wiki/Abstract_syntax_tree

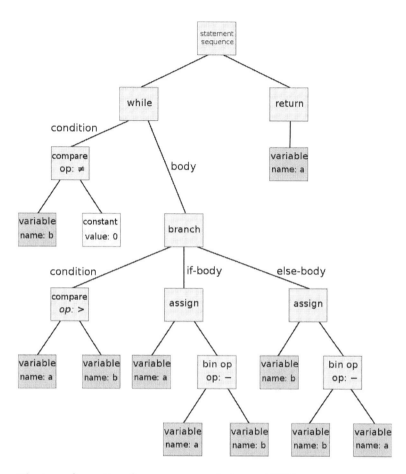

The transformation from source code to an AST, is a very common pattern when processing any type of structured data. The typical workflow is based on *"Creating a parser that converts raw data into an graph-based format, that can then be consumed by an rendering engine"*.

This is basically the process of converting raw data into in strongly typed in-memory objects that can be manipulated programmatically.

Here is a another example from the really cool online tool astexplorer.net[203]:

Built with React, Babel, Font Awesome, CodeMirror, Express, and WebPack | GitHub

Note how in the image above the DOT[204] language raw text was converted into a object tree (which can also be consumed/saved as a json file).

As a developer if you are able to *'see code or raw data as a graph'*, you will have made an amazing paradigm shift which will help you tremendously across your carer.

For example I have used ASTs and custom parsers to:

- write tests that check for what is actually happening in the code (easy when you have access to an object model of the code)
- consume log data which normal 'regex' based parsers struggled to understand
- perform static analysis on code written in custom languages
- transform data dumps into in-memory objects (than can then be easily transformed and filtered)

---

[203]https://astexplorer.net/
[204]https://github.com/DinisCruz/Book_Generation_Z_Developer/blob/master/content/2.mvp-for-gen-z-dev/content/dot-language.md

- create transformed files with slices of multiple source code files (which I called MethodStreams and CodeStreams) - See example below for what this looks like in practice
- perform custom code refactoring (for example to automatically fix security issues in code) - See example below for what this looks like in practice

Refactoring and write code from AST

When building a parser for a particular data source, a key milestone is the round-trip capability, of being able to go from the AST, back to the original text (with no data loss).

This is exactly how code refactoring[205] in IDEs works (for example when you rename a variable and all instances of that variable are renamed).

Here is how this round-trip works:

1. start with *file A* (i.e. the source code)
2. create the AST of *file A*
3. create *file B* as transformation from the AST
4. *file A* is equal to *file B* (byte by byte)

When this is possible, it becomes easy to change code programmatically, since we will be manipulating strongly typed objects without worrying about the creation of syntactic correct source code (which is now a transformation from the AST).

Writing tests using ASTs objects

Once you start to see your source code (or data that you consume) as *'only an AST parser away from being objects you can manipulate'*, a whole word of opportunities and capabilities will open up for you.

---

[205]https://en.wikipedia.org/wiki/Code_refactoring

A good example is how to detect a particular pattern in the source code that you want to make sure occurs in a large number of files, lets say for example that you want to: *"make sure that a particular Authorization (or data validation) method is called on every exposed web services method"*?

This is not a trivial problem, since unless you are able to programmatically write a test that checks for this call, your only options are:

1. write a 'standard document/wiki-page' that defines that requirement, and make sure that all developers read it, understand it, and more importantly, follow it
2. manually check if that standard/requirement was correctly implemented (on Pull Requests code reviews)
3. try to use automation with 'regex' based tools (commercial or open source), and realise that it is really hard to get good results from it
4. fallback on manual QA tests (and Security reviews) to pick up any blind-spots

But, when you have the capability to write tests that check for this requirement, here is what happens:

1. write tests that consume the code's AST to be able to very explicitly check if the standard/requirement was correctly implemented/coded
2. via comments in the test file, the documentation can be generated from the test code (i.e. no extra step required to create documentation for this standard/requirement)
3. run those tests as part of the local build and as part of the main CI pipeline
4. by having a failed test, the developers will know ASAP once an issue has been discovered, and can fix it very quickly

This is a perfect example of how to scale architecture and security requirements, in a way that is embedded within the Software Development Lifecycle.

We need ASTs for legacy and cloud environments

The more your get into ASTs, the more you realise that they are abstractions layers between different layers or dimensions. More importantly they allow the manipulation of a particular layer's data in a programmatic way.

But when you look at the current legacy and cloud environments (the part that we call 'Infrastructure as code'), what you will see are large parts of that ecosystems that today don't have AST parsers to convert their reality into programable objects.

This is a great area of research, where you would focus on creating DSLs (Domain Specific Languages) for either legacy systems or for cloud applications (pick one since each will have complete different sets of source materials). One example of the kind DSL we need is an language to describe and codify the behaviour of Lambda functions (namely the resources they need to execute, and what is the expected behaviour of the Lambda function)

MethodStreams

One of the most powerful examples of AST manipulation I've seen, is the MethodStreams feature that I added to the O2 Platform[206].

With this feature I was able to programmatically create a file based on the call tree of a particular method. This file contained all the source code relevant to that original method (generated from multiple files), and made a massive difference when doing code reviews.

---

[206]http://o2platform.com

To understand why I did this, let's start with the problem I had.

Back in 2010 I was doing a code review of an .Net application that had a million lines of code. But I was only looking at the WebServices methods, which only covered a small part of that codebase (which made sense since those were the methods exposed to the internet). I knew how to find those internet exposed methods, but in order to understand how they worked, I had to look at hundreds of files, which were the files that contained code in the execution path of those methods.

Since in the O2 Platform I already had a very strong C# parser and code refactoring support (implemented for the REPL feature), I was able to quickly write a new module that:

1. starting on web service method X
2. calculated all methods called from that method X
3. calculated all methods called by 2. (recursively)
4. capture the AST objects from all the methods identified by the previous steps
5. created a new file with all the objects from 4.

This new file was amazing, since it contained ONLY the code that I need to read during my security review.

But it got event better, since in this situation, I was able to add the validation RegExs (applied to all WebServices methods) to the top of the file, and add the source code of the relevant Stored Procedures at the bottom of the file.

Some of the generated files had 3k+ lines of code, which was a massive simplification of the 20+ files that contained them (which had probably 50k+ lines of code).

Here is a good example of me being able to do a better job, by having access to a wide set of capabilities and techniques (in this case the ability to programmatically manipulate source code)

This type of AST manipulation is an area of research that I highly recommend for you to focus on (which will also give you a massive toolkit for your day to day coding activities). Btw, If you go down this path, also check out the O2 Platform's **CodeStreams** which are an evolution of the **MethodStreams** technology. CodeStreams will give you a stream of all all variables that are touched by a particular source variable (what in static analysis is called *Taint flow analysis*[207] and *Taint Checking*[208])

Fixing code in real time (or at compilation time)

Another really cool example of the power of AST manipulation is the PoC I wrote in 2011 on *Fixing/Encoding .NET code in real time (in this case Response.Write)*[209], where I show how to programmatically add a security fix to a vulnerable by design method.

Here is what the UI looked like, where the code on the left, was transformed programmatically to the code on the right (by adding the extra `AntiXSS.HtmlEncode` wrapper method)

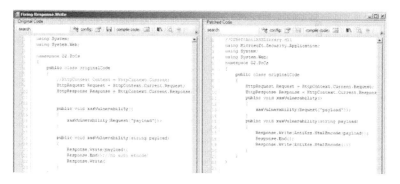

---

[207]http://www.rroij.com/open-access/taint-flow-analysis-for-the-detection-of-bufferoverflow-attacks-.php

[208]https://en.wikipedia.org/wiki/Taint_checking

[209]https://o2platform.wordpress.com/2011/11/07/fixingencoding-net-code-in-real-time-in-this-case-response-write/

Here is the source code that does the transformation and code fix (note the round-trip of code):

```
var csharpAst = text.csharpAst();
foreach(var invocationExpression in csharpAst.CompilationUnit.iNodes<InvocationExpression>())
{
        var memberReference = invocationExpression.TargetObject as MemberReferenceExpression;
        if (memberReference.notNull() && memberReference.MemberName == "Write")
        {
                var className = "AntiXss";
                var methodName = "HtmlEncode";
                var newMemberReference = new MemberReferenceExpression(new IdentifierExpression(className),methodName );
                var newInvocationExpression = new InvocationExpression(newMemberReference);
                newInvocationExpression.Arguments.AddRange(invocationExpression.Arguments);
                invocationExpression.Arguments.Clear();
                invocationExpression.Arguments.Add(newInvocationExpression );
        }
        csharpAst.CompilationUnit.add Using("Microsoft.Security.Application");
}

var patchedCSharpCode = csharpAst.CompilationUnit.csharpCode();
var patchedCSharpFile = patchedCSharpCode.saveWithExtension(".cs");
patchedCode.open(patchedCSharpFile);
```

In 2018, the way to implement this workflow in a developer friendly way, is to automatically create a Pull Request with those extra changes.

Life Patterns

....

Learning

Do you know how to learn?

Learning to learn is one of the most important skills that you can have, and in fact, that is the main skill to learn from school and life. This is ironic, since usually very little time is spent at school and life in learning out to learn.

Learning is like a muscle, the more you do it, the better your become. And just like in sports, there are specific techniques that you can use to learn more efficiently.

As a developer if you are not passionate about learning, you are on the wrong job!

It is not about learning one, or two or three programming languages or development frameworks. You need to learn 10+ languages and be on a constant learning curve. Each language will tech you something new (don't worry, only the first 5 will be hard, after that, the key paradigms will always feel familiar). For example, it is very hard to learn about functional programming until you start coding in Node or in Scala (after banging your head against the wall for a bit, it will click, and you will love its power and ability to write really simple code)

It is about learning new paradigms, about interconnecting your skills. What you learn in one domain, will be applicable in another. For example, being a better musician, artist, athlete, car mechanic or philosopher will make you a better developer

Application Security (AppSec) will take this to another level, since you will be asked to code review in all sorts of languages (which is great, since that is the best way to learn). AppSec focus on how 'it' really works, now just how it behaves.

The reality is that we are in age of the 'professional amateur', where you very rarely have time to really specialize in a particular language or technology. And when you do specialize, if you are not careful, you will be stuck in the past and be the one that is responsible for maintaining the legacy applications.

The best description I've read about how learning occurs is in the Badass: Making Users Awesome[210] book, where Kathy Sierra outlines two key requirements to learn:

- **Practice right** - it is not about how much one practices, but how effective that practice is. This is connected with the idea of being in 'the zone' and it really shows that the real talent is not in being good/excellent in a particular area (for example playing guitar) but it is having the ability and perseverance to practice and learn effectively. Ironically too much talent can actually back fire, since it makes the first part easy and doesn't prepare the student for the hard road ahead. One of my best teachers always said "being good is 1% talent and 99% perspiration'
- **Consume large amounts of good examples** - the very interesting data point here is how much we learn subliminally and by osmosis. Related to the idea that books are much better mediums to learn, when we learn we absorb much more that we think we do. This is why it is so important to keep seeing (and learning from) good examples of what we are are trying to learn. When we see or read from somebody that has gained mastery of a particular topic, we are learning all sorts of things. This is why as a developer is is key that you read lots of source code and try lots of technologies, since each one

---

[210]https://www.amazon.co.uk/Badass-Making-Awesome-Kathy-Sierra/dp/1491919019

will teach you much more than you realise. Remember that all Open Source code is available (usually on GitHub). Spent time on projects you use and dig deep into the source code.

What you really should to be worried about is when you stop learning.

Ironically this can happen the more you move up the company's corporate ladder. There is a big trap of management, which pushes highly technical and proficient developers into 'management' or 'architectural' positions (this is also called the Peters Principle[211] where "employees are promoted to the maximum of their in-competence"). When this happens, these highly knowledgeable professionals have very little time to spend on technical issues, spending most of of their on meetings, spreadsheets and 'non learning activities'

Here are some ideas for how to keep the technical skills up-to-date:

- Be involved as a technical resources (not as a manager) for a couple hours per week in real-world projects (ideally around cloud solutions or incident handling)
- ask the team to create DSLs (Domain Specific Languages) that abstract their work into easy to code components, and then write code on top of those DSLs
- write and review tests (best way to learn is to read source code, specially unit/integration tests, since they tell the story of what is being tested)
- write integration scripts to automate day-to-day tasks (for example using Zapier and AWS Lambdas)

My view is that no matter your role, you must make sure that you remain highly technical, have a deep understanding of what is going on, and always keep learning. Programming is one of the best ways to do this.

---

[211]https://en.wikipedia.org/wiki/Peter_principle

Work in a learning environment

Ideally this learning environment will be part of your job.

If not, then evenings and weekends are a great time to learn, while you find another job that puts learning at the center of their ecosystem

If you are learning things you are passionate about, the extra effort to learn should feel easy, and actually be relaxing.

Be a founder

The single thing that you personally control when you go to work, is your attitude to your work and how you approach it.

One of the concepts that I really like is the idea that you should *"act like one of the founders of the business"*.

Image you where employee #4 and you really cared deeply about the company you currently are working on!

Ask yourself:

"If I was a founder of the company/department/section I work now, with the responsibilities that I have at the moment: "

- *"How would I behave everyday?"*
- *"What needs to be done now, that will make a big difference?"*
- *"What can I do that will help?"*
- *"What would I do differently?"*
- *"What values and principles would I fight for?"*

Hopefully you will get some interesting ideas and actions (from this mental exercise)

The question now is: *"what is stopping you from doing just that?"*

Who is telling you *"Don't do it"*?

At the moment it is just you!

You can even do this for companies that don't employ you. You can contribute to their open source projects, you can write blog posts about them (and use twitter to reach out to key individuals)

You can choose to care about the team that you are currently in, and the work that needs to be done.

The irony is that the more you care and the more you behave like a founder, the more value you usually add and the more valuable you will become for that company.

Being criticized is an privilege

One of the most important life lessons you need to learn, is to how to give and receive feedback. Specially when the feedback is not positive, and it is criticizing something you've said or done.

My view is that a very effective way to learn (and adjust behavior) is to create environments where your friends and colleges are conformable in criticizing your actions (i.e. to provide their views on how you behave and act). This is not easy, and is something that I work hard at it, specially since my high-level of energy can very easily create blind spots in my understanding of the real impact of my actions (see Why do others think that I'm "hard to deal with" and that "I don't listen"[212]).

If you are lucky enough to be in a position where you are criticized, you should see that as a privilege and an asset that you have.

But listening to somebody (and their criticisms) doesn't mean that you have to agree with what they say and do what they tell you to do :)

---

[212]http://blog.diniscruz.com/2012/10/why-do-others-think-that-im-hard-to.html

What it means is that you understand their point of view. Also important is that you let them know that you've acknowledged their feedback and will consider their ideas.

Here are three models I use for the cases when I don't agree with somebody:

- Agree to Disagree[213]
- Disagree and Commit[214].
- Disagree and Ignore

Usually, disagreeing and committing is a much better outcome, since that makes sure that all parties are aligned in the right objective or idea.

Agreeing to Disagree is a close 2nd since that means that you were able to reach a consensus that both don't have the same view on a particular idea/subject/behaviors.

Sometimes, specially in the social media world (or Open Source world) there are tons of people with lots of 'half-baked ideas and criticisms', where the only rational and effective solution is to ignore them (or block them)

Note: always ignore and block trolls and other online personas who are completely irrational, and only bring negativity to the table. They are not worth it, and you will learn nothing from them.

Learn who is your public persona

Part of the exercise is to tune in your understanding of reality, with what is really going on.

You need to build trust relationships with your community, where your friends and colleagues (both up and down the org chart) are

---

[213]https://en.wikipedia.org/wiki/Agree_to_disagree
[214]https://en.wikipedia.org/wiki/Disagree_and_commit

comfortable in telling you what they really think about you and how you behave.

I really like the concept that *"if you want to go fast you can go alone"*, but *"if you want to go far (and have sustainability), you need to work with a team"*.

Nobody creates anything that is valuable by itself. It is always a team effort, and you need to learn how to be an effective team player (regardless of what position you are playing at that moment in time)

One of the key concepts that I have in my mind is the fact *you can't control how somebody will react to your actions*. So don't fight it and use those reactions in your feedback loop, and become a better person, professional and manager.

Myers–Briggs and 16 personalities

Does this means that you need to react differently to different people?

Yes! Absolutely.

A feedback from person A could set a number of alert bells in your head (as in *'... Hummm... I might be going on the wrong direction ...'*), but the exact same feedback from person B could give you a confirmation that you are indeed going on the right direction :)

The way to do this is to reverse-engineer how somebody behaves and think, and apply that filter to what they say. The fact is that people are different and they will react differently to the same situation.

Myers–Briggs Type Indicator[215] is a really good framework to understand this where most people can be split into 8 learning styles:

---

[215]https://en.wikipedia.org/wiki/Myers%E2%80%93Briggs_Type_Indicator

- Extraversion vs Introversion
- Sensing vs Intuition
- Thinking vs Feeling
- Judging vs Perceiving

Another related framework is the _Big Five Personality Traits[216] which maps five factors:

- Openness to experience (inventive/curious vs. consistent/-cautious)
- Conscientiousness (efficient/organized vs. easy-going/care-less)
- Extraversion (outgoing/energetic vs. solitary/reserved)
- Agreeableness (friendly/compassionate vs. challenging/de-tached)
- Neuroticism (sensitive/nervous vs. secure/confident)

---

[216]https://en.wikipedia.org/wiki/Big_Five_personality_traits

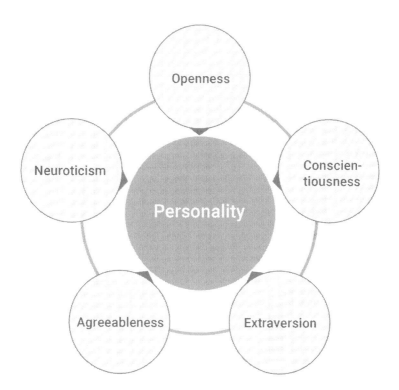

To see both of these frameworks in action see the 16personalities.com[217] website who have merged these two frameworks[218] and come up with with 16 different personalities:

---

[217]https://www.16personalities.com
[218]https://www.16personalities.com/articles/our-theory

Analysts	Confident Individualism	Architect (Assertive), Logician (Assertive)
	People Mastery	Commander (Assertive), Debater (Assertive)
	Constant Improvement	Architect (Turbulent), Logician (Turbulent)
	Social Engagement	Commander (Turbulent), Debater (Turbulent)
Diplomats	Confident Individualism	Advocate (Assertive), Mediator (Assertive)
	People Mastery	Protagonist (Assertive), Campaigner (Assertive)
	Constant Improvement	Advocate (Turbulent), Mediator (Turbulent)
	Social Engagement	Protagonist (Turbulent), Campaigner (Turbulent)
Sentinels	Confident Individualism	Logistician (Assertive), Defender (Assertive)
	People Mastery	Executive (Assertive), Consul (Assertive)
	Constant Improvement	Logistician (Turbulent), Defender (Turbulent)
	Social Engagement	Executive (Turbulent), Consul (Turbulent)
Explorers	Confident Individualism	Virtuoso (Assertive), Adventurer (Assertive)
	People Mastery	Entrepreneur (Assertive), Entertainer (Assertive)
	Constant Improvement	Virtuoso (Turbulent), Adventurer (Turbulent)
	Social Engagement	Entrepreneur (Turbulent), Entertainer (Turbulent)

For reference here is mine :)

123

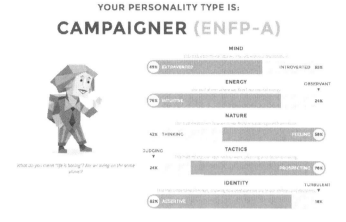

Note that although these frameworks might not be 100% accurate, I found the results I've seen to be quite exact in practice.

Learn about how the mind works

One topic that has really help me to grow and understand better how to work in teams is the amazing Neuroscience and Behavioural research that has been published recently in books like:

- Incognito: The Secret Lives of The Brain[219]
- Predictably Irrational: The Hidden Forces That Shape Our Decisions[220]
- Nudge: Improving Decisions About Health, Wealth and Happiness[221]
- Fish!: A remarkable way to boost morale and improve results[222]

[219]https://www.amazon.co.uk/Incognito-Secret-Lives-Brain-Canons/dp/1782112464
[220]https://www.amazon.co.uk/Predictably-Irrational-Hidden-Forces-Decisions/dp/0007256531/
[221]https://www.amazon.co.uk/Nudge-Improving-Decisions-Health-Happiness/dp/0141040017/
[222]https://www.amazon.co.uk/Fish-remarkable-morale-improve-results/dp/1444792806/

- Freakonomics: A Rogue Economist Explores the Hidden Side of Everything[223]

Importance of diversity and balance in teams

One of the key reasons why a diverse team is so important, is because having teams made of individuals of primarily one type, will invariably create blind spots, promote GroupThink[224] and lead to bad decisions. This is a point that Jane raises in her *InSecurity: Why a Failure to Attract and Retain Women in Cybersecurity is Making Us All Less Safe*[225] book (i.e. having cyber risk decisions being made by a predominately male population does not usually result in the best possible outcome)

Being aware of the team members personalities is a great way to ensure that the right mix or the right balance exists.

Radical Candour

As a framework to think about feedback I really like the ideas presented in the *Radical Candor*[226] book, which provide a mental model based on two main axis of behavior: Care Personally and Challenge directly:

---

[223]https://www.amazon.co.uk/Freakonomics-Economist-Explores-Hidden-Everything/dp/0141019018/
[224]https://en.wikipedia.org/wiki/Groupthink
[225]https://www.amazon.com/InSecurity-Failure-Attract-Retain-Cybersecurity/dp/178133269X
[226]https://www.amazon.com/Radical-Candor-Kickass-Without-Humanity/dp/1250103509

- When you *Care Personally*, but Don't *Challenge directly*: you have *Ruinous Empathy* (meaning that real feedback is not provided until it is usually too late)
- When you Don't *Care Personally* and Don't *Challenge directly*: you have *Manipulative Insincerity* (which is really something you don't want to be involved in)
- When you Don't *Care Personally* but *Challenge directly*: you have *Obnoxious Aggression* (which is not a good way to communicate and is bound to make the recipient very reactive and even aggressive)
- When you *Care Personally* and *Challenge directly*: you have *Radical Candor* (which is the sweet spot, when the message has the maximum opportunity of being listened to)

Note that this is not easy at all to put in practice, *Radical Candor* does required a lot of work and effort from both parties. For example, we usually start by saying *'Ok I want to give you some Radical Candor...'* which is usually a good way to kickstart the conversation and prime all parties for what is going to happen next.

It is not easy to give feedback

Although for some personality types it seems that all they can do is to give feedback (which can also be a defence mechanism to cover up for insecurity), the best feedback you can receive is one that is hard to give. You need to be very humble when receiving feedback and appreciate that it is very hard for the other person to do it (since they are going 'on the record', and in most cases it is easier to not say anything)

Remember that if somebody has something to say to you, but is afraid to say it, or thinks that it wont matter because you will not listen, the real loser in this lack of communication is you (not them).

The worse situation you can be in, is being ignored and not knowing what is really going on. You want to make sure that your colleagues are conformable saying to your face, what they say (or think) behind your back.

Learn to like criticism and use it to measure success

The way I try to cope with criticism and comments, is to view them as positive things and even try to enjoy them (which is not easy at all to do, and it does require a lot of practice and soul searching)

A good mental model is to accept that you will always be criticized, and there will always somebody/somewhere that doesn't like what you have just done, or doesn't understand your point of view. With this in mind, what you need to do is to use the 'what' is being criticized as the benchmark of your progress.

Basically you should measure your evolution by what you are being criticized for. Learn to recognize what are side effects of your current path, and use that feedback to confirm your current trajectory.

Always focus on the ideas

Here is an amazing quote from Eleanor Roosevelt[227]: *"Great minds discuss ideas; average minds discuss events; small minds discuss people"*.

Always focus on *the Idea*, and don't worry about how that was said (*the Event*) and who said it (*The People*)

Music and criticism

One of my first big lessons in the power of listening to the right people for what they say, was when I was playing drums professionally and I realized that the best feedback (and criticism) that we received, was not from other musicians (who could be very objective in what was wrong), but it was from audience members (and long standing fans) who really cared about the band and the music.

I was quite curious on why this happened. Why didn't the most qualified individuals to provide feedback (the musicians or music critics), were the ones that really deserved to be listened to? (in fact some of their comments would fall on the 'ignore' bucket).

Here are some thoughts:

- most musicians are not very good teachers and don't know how to give effective feedback (they usually to much focus on technical aspect of the playing)
- they are not the target audience

---

[227]https://www.brainyquote.com/quotes/eleanor_roosevelt_385439

- (some) could have conflict of interests (and not really be interested in your success or improvement)

Note that this doesn't mean that there wasn't value in those musicians comments, it was just that they needed to be heavily filtered.

On the other hand, the criticisms from the audience, would be much more raw and consumable (if you talk to them and get them to give you real feedback).

Related to this is the fact that what I don't really like is praise and compliments, since after the nth variation of *'you looked/sounded great'*, you don't really learn a lot (and most people will default to vanilla compliments).

Finally the positive feedback that is really, really, really valuable is the feedback from the people that you respect the most (which are usually the ones that give you radical candor).

THAT is usually all that you should be looking for.

THAT moment when one of your heroes (or individuals you really respect) gives you a gentle nod of 'well done , that was good!'.

In your life, you will be on the receiving end of many magic moments like this. Unfortunately most miss it and fail to appreciate them. Make sure you celebrate them as they occur, since nothing else matters (money, success, fame).

In life, always celebrate and enjoy the journey (and don't forget to do the *happy dance* on your milestones and successes).

Because the moment you reach your destination, is the moment you start to look for the next challenge (with a new set of expectations)

Backup your life

Backing up your code (and ideas) is one of the most important patterns that you must master. Your current approach to backups will depend on how much have you lost, and how painful it was.

The reality is that sometime and somewhere in the future, you will lose some of your data (and ideas).

This could be something as simple as a lost laptop, or some data that was deleted by accident, or even an ransomware attack that encrypted all the files in your devices or servers. If you don't have a good strategy and habits for how you do your backups, it is just a matter of time before you have a catastrophic event.

Trust me, there are few things in life more soul destroying and demotivating, than having to re-create something again (that you were happy with and you had spent a lot of time creating). Even worse when you are not able to recreate it, which in a business environment can easily lead to you being fired for lack of due-diligence or negligence.

The solution is to think about where you classify and store your data (and ideas), so that you can come up with strategies that work in your day-to-day activities.

I'm going to provide a number of examples of how I do it, which hopefully will give you some ideas:

- **Secrets Minimisation** - From a security point of view, the less secrets you have the better (and the easier it is to backup the rest). This is where the more you embrace the idea to publish as much of your data (and ideas) as possible, the easier it is to use web based services as your backup medium.
- **Passwords** - A clearly important piece of data not to lose or disclose. My strategy is to pick formulas that I can remember and to use 2FA authentication (like SMS) as much as possible (which dramatically reduce the importance of passwords)
- **Future Self** - Part of my drive to share, is to think that one day in the future, my future self will need it. This is also why I like to Open Source as much as as possible, since it makes sure that as I move jobs, I don't have to start from scratch

(for example what happened with me and the O2 Platform research or the Maturity Model tool I developed recently)

- **Git** - Git is not just a version control which you use when you want to commit to the main repo. I've seen developers that code for days before doing a commit. This is missing a massive trick. Not only during those periods between commits there is a high risk of data loss, the developer is also missing the opportunity to go back to a version created a couple hours ago (which was better than the current one). Basically there is only so much Ctrl-Z can help you. Note that you should be using git to store as much data (and ideas) as possible, since this workflow is not just for source code (another reason why I like to use markdown for content and DOT for graphs)
- **Autosave and Commits** - When using git as a data store, I always enable auto-save on the IDEs so that I never have unsaved text in memory. I then use git commits (and git staging) to really understand what has been changed (and to double check those changes before committing to the target branch). This is very empowering and liberating, since I don't really worry about losing anything
- **GitHub** - I push as much code (and ideas) on GitHub as possible. For example I have repos (some private) that act like document storage and (literally) backups. My expectation is that GitHub's backup strategy is sound and better than mine.
- **DropBox and GDocs** - Same thing for DropBox and Google Docs. I use them to store data and rely (as most companies do) on their security and backups (very important to have 2FA on these accounts and to pay for the commercial versions, which provide features like version control and much more storage)
- **Twitter** - I use twitter as my personal search engine, and use it to store all sort of links and ideas that I might be interested in the future
- **Google** - A great site effect of putting your data (and ideas) online on a public and hyperlinked location (for example

on a blog or slideshare), is that Google (and Web Archive[228] project) will eventually index it (and keep a copy for ever). I actually have used these service's caches to recover ideas that I published ages ago, on a platform or site that has since disappeared!

- **Simulate disaster** - Ask yourself, if you lost your laptop now, how painful it would be? For example at this very moment, the only thing I would lose if my laptop disappeared (or was stolen) would be the text in this chapter (and in about 30m, I wouldn't lose anything, since I will have committed this text into Git and GitHub)
- **External Drives** - For large files and VM (not really much these days) I also have a number of external drives in my house that hold it (although some of the most interesting research VMs, like the ones I was using when developing the O2 Platform, have been moved to dropbox)

Finally, you probably noticed that every time I mentioned code I also added a note about 'ideas'. The reason is that you also need to backup your ideas so that your future self has access to them. The reality is that you will forget about those ideas and the connections that got you there. The only way to make sure they are not lost forever is to publish them into an hyperlinked medium.

You basically need to backup your life!

Please make sure that when (not if) some of your devices lose (or encrypt) your creations, you have a quick and efficient way to recover them.

Talking to yourself digitally

Talking to yourself in an digital way is not a sign of madness :)

---

[228]https://web.archive.org/

It is a sign that you are capturing your ideas, knowledge and workflow.

I do this a lot, since I find that it gives me a way to capture what I'm doing in a format that I can easily access later. I'm hyperlinking my knowledge/ideas and speaking to my future self.

By talking to yourself, I basically mean that you are having digital threads (on git commits, github threads, blogs, twitter or slack) where the main person talking (i.e. adding digital content) is you. You describe a problem you have, you write possible solutions and when you find the answer you document that too.

It is very important to be comfortable in talking to yourself digitally, since it is not easy and it can feel quite awkward. But it is totally worth it, usually the main beneficially of those threads is actually you (I have many examples of years later finding blog posts I wrote where the step-by-step details I posted help me not to have to solve the same problem again). That said one of the loneliest moments you can have is when you have a particular problem and the only thread you find on the Internet is actually you a couple years ago talking about that problem and asking for help (it is in that moment that you realise that you are the only one in the world that cares about that issue :))

Usually the reason why you will not do this is because you think (wrongly) that:

- **Nobody will be interested in this info** - this is wrong. Posting your ideas and workflows will help others to understand your thinking and actions. It leaves your workflow behind, which is where the really learning occurs. The worse part is that if you do document the solution later, when describing a journey from 'A to F', you will describe the final solution as linear A, B,C,D,E and F steps. In fact, in practice when solving the problem the first time, you actually went on an number of tangents which are as interesting and valuable as the final solution. In this 'A to F' example the path you took was actually A,B, G, M,Z, T, E, D and finally the F steps (usually the final solution was not discovered in an linear and in-sequence way)

- **This info is obvious** - caused by the 'curse of knowledge' where now that you understand it, the solution is obvious (except that it wasn't obvious to you before you solved it)
- **I will look stupid by asking this question (and providing the answer)** - There are no stupid questions! If you did not knew the answer then that was a valid question (usually the gap is in the way knowledge is shared and captured in your environment). Everybody was a novice once, and did not know that answer! That said, what can be very annoying and counter-productive are the individuals that keep asking the same question and not learning (so as long as you keep learning, you should share your questions, and when you find them, your answers). In fact a really good side effect (in teams) for sharing simpler questions, is that it lowers the bar of what is a question that can be asked, and it can dramatically increases collaboration and team knowledge propagation.
- **Who am I to say this** - caused by 'impostor syndrome' where you are your worse enemy

The future needs you

Sometimes the future just doesn't happen! It needs people like you to make the difference.

Re-enforcing the concept that what matters is not ideas but energy and focus in execution, there are a number of ideas that although brilliant, we still need the right individuals at the right place in order for them to become a reality.

This happens in all fields (for example there is a great interview by Elon Musk where he talks about how the concorde and moon landings are good examples of us going backwards in technological capabilities).

On the developing/coding world, in addition to the WallbyJS (real-time unit test execution and code-coverage visualisation) that I cannot understand why all IDEs do not replicate and deeply integrate those capabilities in their engines, another amazing example is the **Zoetrope (Interacting with the Ephemeral Web)** research by Adobe.

This research was published in this YouTube video[229], and it shows a working real-time time machine for web pages (and other content).

This research transformed the Ephemeral[230] and 'no-past' nature of web pages, into a multi-dimensional graph, where the previous versions of a page's content can be visualised, transformed and analysed in all sorts of ways (check out the video and you will be blown away).

Given how powerful this idea is, the interesting question is "Why hasn't it evolved!".

My view is that because there is a significant amount of research and technology required to reach the workflow shown in that video, and the fact that the technology and ideas where not released under an Open Source license (or Creative Commons), any new attempts would have to start from scratch (since it clearly looks like Adobe did not continued the research projects)

Also important is that an individual's vision and an sustainable economic model matter (i.e. someone who understand the problem and someone who is funding the research). Although the key concepts are clearly shown in the video and easy to understand, in the last 10 years we had not had an individual (or team) with the right energy and drive that has decided to replicate this research into an Open Source environment, and built a strong community around it.

---

[229]https://www.youtube.com/watch?v=7C-B7qdClak
[230]https://en.wiktionary.org/wiki/ephemeral

I'm very frustrated by this lack of development, since there are tons of areas in Application Security where this kind of anti-ephemeral technology would be massively important.

Gen Z dev, if you are looking for a place to start replicating this idea, here is one for you:

Create a tool/website to search and visualise the git files history (for example how to do a search across previous versions of files)

That is not a problem that has been solved today, and not only you would let a lot about how git works, you would be creating a tool very useful to you and the development community. As an example that would allow for the easily discovery of secrets stored in git repos that have been 'deleted' using commits (which means that the secrets still exist in that repo and are available to anybody that can clone it)

Pick a vision and be the one that makes the difference

Part of your path as a Gen Z developer, is to find something that you are really passionate for which you can execute. The win-win scenario is when you pick an idea that either is quite new (like chaos engineering) or has been around for a while but the momentum has been lost. For example the Zoetrope mentioned here, or SAST technology (Static analysis of software/applications/infrastructure for finding security issues)

13831833R00081

Printed in Great Britain
by Amazon